Mark Crosfell –
in appreciation of your very
kind & generous help –

Temperance, Therapy & Trilobites

Dr Ralph Grindrod: Victorian Pioneer

Janet Grierson

Janet Grierson

Cora Weaver
Malvern
2001

Published by Cora Weaver, 4 Hall Green, Malvern, Worcs
WR14 3QX, England

© Malvern Civic Society

Typeset and printed by Aldine Press,
Barnards Green Road, Malvern, Worcs. WR14 3NB

ISBN 1 873809 42 5

Contents

Illustrations

Front Cover: Dr Ralph Grindrod. (Etching based on photo. From P.T.Winskill: *The Temperance Movement and its Workers*)

Back Cover: The author. (Photo courtesy of *Malvern Gazette*)

Preface

When I was collecting material for my recent book *Dr Wilson and his Malvern Hydro* I came across a number of references to Dr Wilson's contemporary, Dr Ralph Barnes Grindrod. His dynamic personality aroused my curiosity and led to the writing of this book.

Dr Grindrod was a pioneer in a variety of enterprises. As a doctor in Manchester he became convinced that "the demon drink" was a root cause of the ill-health of many of his patients. He decided to give up his lucrative practice and over a period of six years he travelled throughout the country lecturing to vast crowds on the medical aspects of temperance.

At the age of thirty-nine he settled in Malvern at Townshend House (now the Music School of Malvern College). Here he adopted the still fairly innovative practice of the Water Cure, but used it alongside other treatments, including hyperbaric therapy which was as yet virtually unknown in England.

As proprietor and editor of *The Malvern Advertiser* he gave the town its first local newspaper, and for ten years used its pages to influence public opinion on medical, social and industrial issues, and in general to promote the welfare of Malvern. His prolific output of books and pamphlets was devoted to the same causes.

In addition to all these activities he made his mark on the scientific world. His museum, with its unique collection of fossils, was built up at a time when the cutting of the railway through the Malvern Hills opened up a treasure store for geologists. His collection was acquired in 1882 by the Oxford University Museum of Natural History.

Dr Grindrod's interests and contacts were so wide that my debt to others in collecting material for this book has been considerable. My thanks are due to the trustees and staff of the following institutions: the Guildhall Library; Imperial College Geology Library (especially Ms Lesley Preece); the Institute of Alcohol Studies, Alliance House; Lambeth Palace Library; Livesey Library, University of Central Lancashire; London University (Goldsmith Collection); Malvern

College; Malvern Museum; Malvern Priory; the Natural History Museum; the Oxford University Museum of Natural History (and especially Mr Philip Powell,who provided much of the material on Dr Grindrod's museum); the Public Libraries of Manchester, Worcester and Malvern (especially in the latter to Mr Barber and all the staff for their unfailing kindness during the long period when I have been working there); the Record Offices of Cheshire, Newport and Worcester; the Wellcome Unit for the History of Medicine, Manchester University (especially Mrs Joan Mottram, who helped me not only with Dr Grindrod's Manchester period, but also used her holiday to do research in the Isle of Wight).

I am also grateful to the following who have helped in a variety of ways: Miss M. Braithwaite; Professor R. Fortey; Mr A. Gaynor-Smith; Mr D. George; Mr R. Hall-Jones; Miss J. Hebden; Canon P. J. Hunt; Mr B. J. Powell; Dr S. Richards; Mr N. Rosser; Dr A. Rushton; Professor H.S.Torrens; Mr A.Turner-Bishop; and Dr K. Webb.

Most of all I am indebted to the following: Mr Mark L. Crosfill for his generosity in sharing with me much of the material he collected for his article on Dr Grindrod in the *Journal of Medical Biography*; Dr Nancy Ball for her work at the Cheshire Record Office and her visits to Swettenham cum Kermincham; Miss Marie Eamer who has been a strong support and provided the book with an index; Professor Philip Grierson, who has throughout taken an interest in the work and has made many visits to the Cambridge University Library to deal with my queries; Mrs Valerie Norris who has combed the London libraries for information on Dr Grindrod's temperance travels; and Ms Cora Weaver for attending so helpfully to all the practical details involved in preparing the MS for publication.

1

Distinction for a Doctor

On April 27,1855, a Malvern doctor, Ralph Barnes Grindrod, knelt at the altar rails in Lambeth Palace Chapel to receive from the Archbishop a Lambeth degree. Tall, distinguished in appearance, with a well-groomed curly beard and side whiskers, his kindly expression would have marked him out as a suitable candidate for the role of Father Christmas. On this occasion he was the recipient of an honour that he was to prize highly for the rest of his life.

From 1583, with the passing of the Ecclesiastical Licences Act, commonly known as the Peter Pence Act, certain powers previously exercised by the Pope were transferred by Henry Vlll to the Archbishop of Canterbury. Amongst these was the power to confer degrees. This authority is referred to in the form of service used for the ceremony: "The Archbishops of Canterbury, enabled by the public Authority of the Law, do enjoy and long have enjoyed, the Power of Conferring Degrees and Titles of Honour upon those considered deserving of such recognition." Why should Dr Grindrod have been singled out for a distinction conferred only rarely on a medical practitioner?

The archaic wording of Dr Grindrod's diploma does not throw much light on the problem: "John Bird, by Divine Providence Archbishop of Canterbury, Primate of All England and Metropolitan by authority of Parliament lawfully empowered for the purposes herein to our beloved in Christ, Ralph Barnes Grindrod of Malvern in the county of Worcester, Gentleman, Health and Grace in Jesus Christ our Saviour. We therefore being invested with the authority aforesaid, and following the example of our predecessors, have judged it expedient that you whose proficiency in the study of physic, uprightness of life, and purity of morals are manifest unto us, be dignified with the degree of Doctor of Physic, and we do by these presents, so far as in us lies and the laws of this realm do allow, accordingly create you an actual Doctor of Physic, and we do also admit you into the number of Doctors of Physic of this realm, the oaths hereunder written having been by us or our Master of the Faculties first required of you and by you taken."

Dr Grindrod had indeed shown "proficiency in the study of physic" and was a competent doctor with well established practices, first in Manchester and now in Great Malvern. There would have been many who would have been happy to vouch for his "uprightness of life and purity of morals." In fact one of his pious patients some years later was to contrast him favourably and somewhat quaintly with another prominent Malvern doctor on the grounds that the latter, though "a very clever man is not worthy of example in all respects. He never lives with his wife nor yet goes to any place of worship."

Such qualities, however, were hardly enough to have earned him this special recognition. Clearly there must have been more than this to bring him to the attention of the archbishop.

Before his appointment to Canterbury John Bird Sumner had been Bishop of Chester. Ralph Grindrod was born in a Cheshire parish. He was also baptised there and grew up as a devout member of the Anglican Church. A candidate for a Lambeth degree had normally to be sponsored by two beneficed clergymen. But as Dr Grindrod pointed out on one occasion this would hardly have been necessary in his case as the archbishop knew him well and "was willing to ordain me as a clergyman of a church in whose pale I was born and in whose membership I am likely to live and die".

Instead of becoming a clergyman, however, his life had taken a different turn. He had in fact already found another vocation in addition to the practice of medicine. Appalled by the drunkenness that was ruining the lives of so many of his patients, he espoused the cause of temperance with a single-minded zeal that was to earn for him the title "the great medical apostle of temperance". Not only did he promote it in his early days in Manchester, but for over six years he travelled up and down the country on what he called his medical mission. During the three to four days he stayed in each place, he addressed audiences, sometimes numbering several thousand, on the medical aspects of temperance, and always ended the lectures with an appeal to his listeners to take a pledge of total abstinence.

But his concern for the welfare of his patients did not stop there. Alive to the fact that the sufferings of so many sprang from the unhealthy and even cruel conditions in which they lived and worked, many of his lectures, pamphlets and other writings were directed towards those who had it in their power to better the lot of the poorer members of society. By the time of the Lambeth presentation he had settled in Great Malvern to work alongside the doctors already established there, and this stable background enabled him to pursue his work for social reform. The large house needed for his practice provided a centre for promoting these various causes, while as proprietor and editor of a local newspaper he was in an ideal position to influence public opinion.

One can see why the many interests of Dr Grindrod might have caused him to be singled out for recognition by the archbishop. Unlike many of the Anglican clergy of that period Dr Sumner was himself a teetotaller and a strong supporter of the temperance movement. He was also sensitive to the darker side of the industrial revolution which had been brought home to him when he visited the Manchester area of his diocese, and would have appreciated Dr Grindrod's exposure of the sufferings endured by so many women and children, particularly the sempstresses whom he designated in his writings as "slaves of the needle." Whatever the reasons for the conferring of this degree, it is clear that it was deeply appreciated by Dr Grindrod, for to him it represented official appreciation of the value of the work to which he had devoted so many years of his life.

Dr Grindrod, who was in his mid-forties at the time of the Lambeth award, was born on May 19,1811, in Kermincham,[1] a small hamlet in Cheshire, in the parish of Swettenham cum Kermincham. The Grindrod family came originally from Lancashire, the name being derived from that of a hamlet in that county.[2] His parents James and Mary Grindrod farmed their own land, but spent part of the year in the township of Chorlton Row (from 1832 called Chorlton-upon-Medlock) where they had business interests. When the boy was still quite young the family left Kermincham to settle in town and took up residence in Grosvenor Street.

Kermincham was in a remote rural area consisting of two or three substantial properties, a few farms and the whole held together by a network of narrow winding lanes. The largest of these properties was Kermincham Hall, built in the early eighteenth century by Roger Mainwaring whose family crest witnessed to their involvement in the Crusades. The house was situated within a small park enclosed by high brick walls which must have been an incentive to the local children to show off their climbing skills. Kermincham, which had Swettenham Brook meandering through its fields as it flowed into the River Dane, was good agricultural land, and to-day it is still sought after as one of the places where wild daffodils grow in profusion. It was an ideal place for small children, and Ralph and his older brother Thomas took full advantage of all that it had to offer. In Ralph's case it laid the foundation for a life-long interest in every aspect of the natural world. He was later to become a Fellow of the Linnaean Society and the Royal Geographical and Geological Societies. In Malvern he took an active part in the Naturalists' Field Club.

The nearby village of Swettenham had a slightly larger population than that of Kermincham. Central to the village was the parish church of St Peter, approached through a curiously shaped oval churchyard. Dating originally from the thirteenth century it was a timber framed building, whose nave and chancel when they fell into disrepair in the early eighteenth century, were completely encased in brick. Two additions were made at this time: the Mainwaring chapel dedicated to the Kermincham family of that name who had been associated with the church for many hundreds of years and the tower at the west end with its three bells.

At the time of Ralph's baptism the Rev Caleb Bradshaw was its rector, and he was succeeded in 1814 by Thomas Swettenham. Here young Ralph and his family would have attended matins Sunday by Sunday, listening to the lengthy sermons customary at that period and joining in the responses and psalms with music provided by a small local band. He may well have known the violinist Samuel Newton whose fiddle is still to be seen hanging in a case on the north wall.

Dr Grindrod's writings contain no reference to his early education, but it is likely that he and his brother would have been educated privately at least while the family lived in the country. A good grounding in the classics would have been essential for anyone whose ambition was to enter the medical profession, and it is clear that Ralph was not only proficient in Greek and Latin, but also had an extensive knowledge of history, geography, divinity, literature, mathematics and science. Writing came easily to him and he was to become a prolific author and successful newspaper editor. Never at a loss for words, he was to prove himself an extremely able and witty lecturer, with a gift for oratory and skill in repartee. An intelligent and precocious child, his education was such that it enabled him to enter on a course of medical studies when he was not yet thirteen.

Owing to a seven year gap in their ages the two brothers could not have been educated together, and when Ralph was still only six Thomas was apprenticed to a Congleton physician, James Mills Woolfender. His medical training included six months at the Edinburgh Royal Infirmary and he qualified for the licentiateship of the Society of Apothecaries on February 19, 1824. With an admired older brother launched on a medical career it is hardly surprising that Ralph followed in his footsteps at the earliest possible moment. In fact, by conniving with his brother's act of falsifying the entry of his apprentice's age, the young lad entered upon his career earlier than was officially allowed.

2

The Industrial Scene

It must have been with mixed feelings that young Ralph Grindrod exchanged the familiar sights and sounds of the Cheshire countryside for life in a busy industrial town.

Manchester in the early nineteenth century was a very different place from the Manchester we know to-day. It was not in any sense a homogeneous city, but rather an enormous parish consisting of a cluster of thirty overgrown villages or townships centring on what is now the cathedral. The outer districts which were purely agricultural stretched from the Pennine moors down to the Mersey. Nearer the centre were some desirable residential areas to which the more prosperous businessmen moved when the central part became increasingly noisome and overcrowded. It is interesting, for example, to note that when Manchester in 1839 was given its own bench of JPs only five out of thirty lived in the centre; the rest, with one exception, had houses in the inner townships, within four miles or less of their place of work. Four of these JPs lived in Chorlton-upon-Medlock, the township to which Ralph's parents had moved.

James Wheeler's *Manchester: its Political, Social and Commercial History*, published in 1836, presents an interesting picture of Chorlton in these early years of the nineteenth century. His observations are backed up by detailed statistics. The rapidity of development was a marked feature of all these inner townships. The figures for Chorlton were: 1801, 675; 1811, 2581; 1821, 8209; and 1831, 20,569. His comment on this was "a town has actually been created within a few years by the erection of factories." While cotton spinning is commonly associated with the Manchester area it is clear that the industrial scene was much more comprehensive. The 1832 Act for regulation of the police of Chorlton-upon-Medlock proposed that "cotton-spinners, dyers, printers, machine-makers, velvet-dressers, brewers, bakers, smiths, founders, boiler-makers, soap-boilers, pipe-makers, and other artificers and manufacturers, making use of fires casting up large quantities of smoke or flame, may be compelled to construct their chimneys of any height, not exceeding thirty yards, that the Commissioners shall direct; and fire places and chimneys for engines are to be constructed so as best to consume their smoke. In case of the formation of Town's Gas Works, one-half of the profit may be expended in improvements." An 1831 census of the townships constituting the parish of Manchester notes that Chorlton had 1900 men employed in the cotton and silk manufactures, and that there were "1900 workers in iron and brass (in foundries and so forth)." Further analysis indicated that out of a total population of 20,569 only 41 labourers were in agriculture. Manufacture and machine-making accounted for 1898 persons; retail trade or handicraft as masters or workmen employed 789; the number for agricultural workers was 843; and "capitalists, bankers, professional or other educated men" numbered 1080. The better class homes were situated along spacious streets to the south of the township with All Saints Church (built 1820) catering for their special needs. Richard Cobden (best known as leader of the Anti-Corn Law League) campaigned for a charter to incorporate the townships into a municipal borough of Manchester. In one of his pamphlets he argues for the good sense of such a move, citing Chorlton in particular: "The population of Chorlton are so entirely connected with, and indeed dependent upon, Manchester, by business ties, that it is impossible the two can have separate interests . . . As the owners and occupiers of property the two townships are essentially the same, and as the equalisation of the two rates could only increase the one by diminishing the other, no loss could be suffered by such parties, any more than the taking of money from one pocket to put it in another would constitute a robbery. The same arguments apply, prospectively at least, to the clerks and other junior members of the trading community residing in Chorlton, who, though they are not at present occupying warehouses or offices in Manchester, are enjoying the prospect of doing so and who are too enlightened to oppose an amelioration in local government, in which they are probably beyond all others ultimately interested."[1]

While Cobden's references suggest a pleasant suburban environment, it should not be thought that the district was without its mean streets and slum quarters. The Medlock and the Irwell into which it flowed were very different rivers from the pure waters of the River Dane of Ralph Grindrod's old home. Nowhere in the vicinity of Manchester could escape the effects of the industrial revolution. Alexis de Tocqueville,[2] a French aristocrat, who visited it in 1835, comments on these rivers: "Below the hills a narrow river (the Irwell), which flows slowly to the Irish sea. Two streams (the Medlock and the Irk) wind through uneven ground and after a thousand bends, flow into the river. Three canals made by man unite their tranquil, lazy waters at the same point. On this watery land, which nature and art have contributed to keep damp are scattered palaces and hovels." De Tocqueville goes on to describe the miserable conditions of these hovels, but a still more graphic picture is given by Elizabeth Gaskell who knew the Manchester slums from her own personal observation. In her book *Mary Barton* she tells how in a time of recession when sickness ravaged the poor areas, George Wilson took John Barton to visit his friends the Davenports. Passing through unpaved streets, with a centre gutter along which flowed every type of sewage, they came to "a small area, where a person standing would have his head about one foot below the level of the street, and might at the same time, without the least motion of his body, touch the window of the cellar and the damp muddy wall right opposite. You went down one step even from the foul area into the cellar in which a family of human beings lived. It was very dark inside. The window panes of many of them were stuffed with rags, which was reason enough for the dusky light that pervaded the place even at mid-day . . . on going into the cellar inhabited by Davenport, the smell was so foetid as almost to knock the two men down. Quickly recovering themselves, as those inured to such things do, they began to penetrate the thick darkness of the place, and to see three or four little children rolling on the damp, nay wet, brick floor, through which the stagnant, filthy moisture of the street oozed up; the fire-place was empty and black; the wife sat on her husband's lair, and cried in the dank loneliness."[3]

The rapid industrialisation of the area was largely responsible for this situation, with dwellings standing cheek by jowl with the mills and factories. De Tocqueville comments on the impact made on him by the sight of so many of these in so confined a space: "Thirty or forty factories rise on top of the hills I have just described. Their six stories tower up; their huge enclosures give notice from afar of the centralisation of industry. The wretched dwellings of the poor are scattered around them." What could be seen from afar was much worse when the centre of all this industry was reached. "Look up," he says, "and all around this place you will see the huge palaces of industry. You will hear the noise of furnaces, the whistle of steam. These vast structures keep air and light out of the human habitations which they dominate; they envelope them in perpetual fog." He continues: "A sort of black smoke covers the city. The sun seen through it is a disc without rays. Under this half-light 300,000 human beings are ceaselessly at work. A thousand noises disturb this dark damp labyrinth, but they are not at all the ordinary sounds one hears in great cities. The footsteps of a busy crowd, the crunching wheels of machinery, the shriek of steam from boilers, the regular beat of the looms, the heavy rumble of carts, those are the noises from which you can never escape in the sombre half-light of these streets."

The mid 1820s saw particular hardship throughout the whole area. Trade was stagnating, while more and more sophisticated machinery was replacing manpower, and the operatives who were laid off were liable to turn to desperate remedies. Factories, especially those engaged in weaving, were attacked, and in some cases there was resort to arson. Shops selling provisions were looted by the starving populace. Some attempts were made to provide relief. Thousands were assisted through the distribution of soup and other basic foods, clothing was supplied from government stores, and alternative employment was offered in the form of road making. But none of these measures could do much to alleviate the poverty, and with poverty came a worsening of housing conditions and a lowering of resistance to sickness.

An institution in which the Grindrod brothers were closely involved was the Chorlton Row Dispensary which was set up in 1826. Previously the district had been served by the Manchester Royal Infirmary, but with the hugely expanding population of the parish of Manchester its dispensary services were proving totally inadequate. With the Royal Infirmary unable to undertake further commitments, the Chorlton Select Vestry, who administered the Poor Law, accepted responsibility for contributing to the payment for paupers, while the rest of the cost of a dispensary had to be met by voluntary contributions from local subscribers. Such subscribers, many of them mill owners and factory owners, but including also a number of professional and other well-to-do citizens, were in return given the right to purchase treatment for their own nominees. The Birley family, who were the largest mill owners in the district, were prominent in the venture, and Hugh Birley who led the charge of the local volunteer cavalry in the notorious Peterloo massacre of 1819 became the dispensary's first president. During its first four years the dispensary was housed free of charge in rooms in the Chorlton Police Offices, and later with the passing of the Chorlton Improvement Act of 1832 it was housed in the Town Hall.

Physicians and surgeons in Chorlton and neighbourhood awaited the establishment of the new institution with great interest, for appointments to dispensary posts could give them a prominence that might be very influential in their subsequent medical careers. One of these was Ralph Grindrod's brother Thomas who had a practice in Oxford Street. Aged twenty-two and only recently qualified, he must have felt his chances of one of the two surgical appointments were remote. Out of four applicants, however, he was the one selected, to the discomfiture of one of his rivals William Johns who commented later on "the considerable period" he had already served the poor of Chorlton. Perhaps Mr Johns took some comfort from the fact that when Thomas Grindrod resigned some four years later the post was offered to his former rival. Thomas's decision to retire from this exacting appointment to enjoy instead the greater freedom of general practice may have been influenced by his marriage in 1828 to Mary

Ann Newton. The dispensary appears to have had no regrets that their original appointment had been offered to one so young and inexperienced, for the 1831 Report records their gratitude for his "very valuable services and unwearied attention during the time he has held the appointment of surgeon."

3

The Medical Student

On March 1, 1824, Ralph Grindrod was apprenticed to his brother Thomas to begin a course of training that was to lead to his qualification for the licentiateship of the Society of Apothecaries.

The details given in the court of examiners entry books pose a problem. No date of birth is given, but his baptism is entered as October 29, 1808. In the Swettenham church records, however, the baptism entry is May 19, 1811, and this coincides with his date of birth as given by P.T.Winskill,[1] the chief early historian of the temperance movement, and it is also inscribed on his gravestone. There can be little doubt that this date is correct, which shows that he must have managed to circumvent the regulations that an indenture of apprenticeship could not be completed before the age of twenty-one. His brother would presumably have furnished the information to the Society of Apothecaries, while Ralph may well have felt that if he had satisfied the examiners on their medical requirements the question of age was immaterial!

At the time of his apprenticeship there was no university in Manchester, but Dr Grindrod never regretted that he had done his training there rather than at one of the universities. While he appreciated the cachet that went with a university degree, he was convinced that Manchester offered opportunities that were more relevant to the needs of general practice. When on the occasion of his Lambeth degree a snide comment was made in the local paper owned by another Malvern doctor, who prided himself on his own Edinburgh degree, he answered the question of why he did not take a similar course with the incisive comment: "1.As a general practitioner I did not need it. 2.When I determined to devote myself to a more special practice I did not care for it, and also because it would have been entirely useless." For good measure he added that however honourable a degree in Scotland might be it had not even been a legal document in England only three to four years earlier. He then went on to expand on the exceptional opportunities offered by Manchester. In this opinion he was not alone, for James Wheeler also enlarges on its merits and supports this view with a quotation from the unsolicited testimonial of an examining body before a committee of the House of Commons: "No class of pupils is better prepared than those who have been educated solely at Manchester."

With his pragmatic approach to medicine Dr Grindrod valued highly the three and a half years' experience which he gained as his brother's apprentice in the Chorlton Row Dispensary, as it gave him an insight into the treatment of large numbers of patients particularly from the poorer districts. When the dispensary opened in 1826 it admitted over 1800 patients, many of them as outpatients. The numbers dropped in 1828, with 1534 patients being admitted, of whom 550 were visited at home; and in 1829 the number was 1557, of whom 510 were visited at home. Because of the many factories in the area accidents accounted for nearly one tenth of the total figures, while the rest would have been miscellaneous types of sickness, especially fever. Where possible the latter cases were visited at home. Because of the poor housing conditions in parts of the district, with people living in overcrowded buildings and damp cellars, breathing in foul air, and unable to afford adequate nourishment, epidemics flourished. This was particularly so among the Irish settlers, many of whom were living in the waterlogged areas near the Medlock. Dysentery, typhus, and gastro-enteric diseases were especially common in the summer months; the winter regularly brought its harvest of catarrhal problems such as asthma, pleurisy, pneumonia and phthisis, while rheumatic complaints were always endemic. There was no special provision for children at the dispensary, and most of those suffering from the usual children's ailments such as measles, whooping cough, chicken pox and the complications that so often followed such infectious diseases were treated at home.

In addition to the experience gained as a student at the Chorlton Dispensary, a considerable period of his apprenticeship was taken up with attendance at lectures in the Manchester medical schools. He seems to have shown a particular interest in anatomy and physiology, including anatomical demonstrations, and in these fields of study he became better qualified than his brother. Probably this was because he had the unique opportunity of having Joseph Jordan as his teacher. Jordan, who had been a surgeon in the Royal Lancashire militia and later the regular army, had set up a practice in Manchester in 1812 which he combined with teaching anatomy. At the time of Ralph's apprenticeship he had founded a school of medicine in a purpose-built house on the corner of Mount Street and Albert Square. Although his tall and dignified appearance gave the initial impression of unapproachability, in fact his strong sense of humour and infectious laugh relieved the most demanding sessions in the classroom. It was said of him that his lively lectures "mixed dry anatomical details with anecdotes and jokes and interesting physiological views," so that "nothing was so dry and dull but he would make it interesting." As a surgeon he showed great skill, with a reputation as "a good clinician, and a cool operator, priding himself on the steadiness of his hand." His early experience as an army surgeon led to his devising a new method of dealing with artificial joints that was simple and more effective than any currently in use.

The success of Joseph Jordan's anatomical demonstrations attracted large numbers of students, which sometimes created problems because of the difficulty of obtaining corpses. In earlier years he had on one occasion been fined £20 for his dealings with a resurrectionist who had been caught rifling a grave. But he was determined that his pupils would not be hindered in their work of dissection and eventually found methods of procuring corpses without falling foul of the law. In fact he and his colleague Thomas Turner were able to boast that corpses were easy to get in Manchester and that they were able to supply them to medical schools in Edinburgh and London.

If as a young student Ralph Grindrod held the same views on drink and tobacco as he did in later years, he would have appreciated Jordan's stance on these matters. Even when entertaining important visitors Jordan refused ever to allow alcohol at his table, and smoking was also taboo although he did have a weakness for taking snuff.

1. Owens College.   6. The Chatham Street School.

2. Jordan's House.   7. The first Infirmary Building (1752-55)

3. Jordan's Dissecting Room.   8. The second Infirmary Building (1755-1908).

4. The Mount Street School.   9. Chetham's Hospital.

5. The Pine Street School.   10. The Cathedral.

11. The Marsden Street School.

Plan showing location of early hospital buildings, Manchester

15

Another lecturer at Joseph Jordan's School was Thomas Fawdington, who also held an appointment as man-midwife to the Manchester Lying-in-Charity which had been set up in 1790. There is no evidence that Ralph Grindrod qualified in midwifery which anyway was not regarded as essential for the general practitioner, but he probably attended his lectures on anatomy and physiology. What may have had a greater influence on him was the latter's interest in establishing a museum of morbid anatomy, which specialised in diseases of the bones and mucous membranes. In his later career Thomas Fawdington was elected to the staff of the Manchester Royal Infirmary, and the contents of his museum which had been valued at £2000 was eventually bought by this institution for £210. Dr Grindrod's medical museum in Malvern may have owed something to his early contact with this notable collector.

A school of medicine which also competed for students at this time was Thomas Turner's in Pine Street. From later references to his medical training it would seem that Ralph sought out the best teachers of each particular discipline regardless of their place of work. The Pine Street School, which later enjoyed the title "The Manchester Royal School of Medicine and Surgery", was established in 1825, and here Ralph had the privilege of studying chemistry under Dr John Dalton, the distinguished mathematician and chemist who was already notable as the first propounder of the modern chemical atomic theory. Another teacher at Pine Street, who subsequently became one of Ralph's great friends and his personal physician, was Dr James L Bardsley. Dr Bardsley was honorary physician to the Royal Infirmary from 1823, and from 1825 he taught physic, materia medica and botany at the Pine Street School. Ralph would have known his father too as he was consulting physician to the Chorlton Row Dispensary when it first opened.

Ralph Grindrod's apprenticeship came to an end with his qualification for the licentiateship of the Society of Apothecaries on January 7, 1830. The details of his course given in the court of examiners entry book are fairly sketchy, but they include his three and a half years at the Chorlton Dispensary, and confirm that he attended lectures on chemistry, materia medica, anatomy and physiology, anatomical demonstrations, theory and practice of medicine, and botany. In the case of three subjects, anatomy and physiology, anatomical demonstrations, and theory and practice of medicine, his lectures extended to two sessions. These would have been basic to his future career in general practice, besides ensuring that his approach to his medical temperance mission had a genuinely scientific basis.

4

Temperance Pioneer

When Ralph Grindrod completed his medical course he left Manchester and set up a practice in Runcorn, with his private residence in Halton Castle. Runcorn at that time bore little resemblance to the busy industrial town of to-day, and he must have appreciated the pleasanter living conditions that it offered. Pigott's Directory of 1822 comments on "the fine air, the pleasantness of the neighbourhood (particularly Halton Castle) and the exhilarating effects of the busy scene on the river, which had made it a bathing resort." Although in general practice, his work included appointments as medical officer to a number of working men's clubs. He has left us no information on what drew him to Runcorn, but it is possible that some of these clubs may have had a connexion with the quarries of high grade hard sandstone which were a main source of employment in the town.

T.Rigby's *A History of Runcorn and Weston* records a reference in the 1821 census to Grindrod's quarries on Hill Brow in Weston. Earlier than this there was a co-partnership in these quarries of Messrs Heatherington, Grindrod, and Edwards & Allison; and Pigott's Directory of 1822 lists as tradesmen, Grindrod and Heatherington, stone merchants, and Timothy Grindrod, stone merchant.

The 1831 census omits any mention of a Grindrod at the quarries, and Pigott's Directory of 1834 shows the ownership now with Heatherington. If there had been a Grindrod family connexion, as seems likely, it would probably account for Ralph's decision to leave Manchester, where his reputation as a keen, industrious and talented student could have guaranteed him a successful career.

His stay in Runcorn lasted about two years, and during this time he became increasingly aware of the devastating effect that drunkenness was having on the health of his patients and the well-being of their families. He had of course known of this while a student in Manchester, but now that he had his own practice he felt responsible for using his influence to tackle the problem. To understand the total dedication of pioneers like himself one needs to appreciate the situation at that time.

The seriousness of the drink problem in the early nineteenth century was by no means confined to the working classes. No section of society was unaffected. To drink oneself under the table was an accepted mark of manliness, and the ladies were expected to withdraw after dinner so that the gentlemen could give free rein to their indulgence. Small wonder that gout figured largely among the diseases of the wealthy. But the ladies drank too, though perhaps more discreetly, and often what began as a prescription of gin or brandy for painful periods or frequent confinements led to an addiction. They had their drugs too, and the combination of laudanum and spirits must have been a deadly potion. With no aspirin available for the relief of pain and no anaesthetics to make surgery tolerable, spirits had a widely accepted place among medical remedies.

With the appalling conditions of life in the cities and no opportunities available for healthy recreation, strong drink also became the refuge of working people. It provided them with warmth, protected them from pain and enabled them for a time to forget their miseries. Soft drinks were not the alternative that they can be to-day. Drinking water was scarce and in slum districts dangerously polluted. Because of heavy taxation tea and coffee were expensive in the early years of the century and few of the poorer citizens could afford this luxury. Until the reduction of tax brought about by the Beer Act of 1830 made this drink more readily available, gin had been the poor man's standby. Not only was it relatively cheap, but the gin palace with its lights and convivial atmosphere provided a welcome escape from the sordidness of the slums.

For rich and poor alike strong drink was a feature of every business and social occasion. Rents were paid in the inn or tavern. It was the normal location for auctions, and various sellers of merchandise set up their stalls either inside or immediately outside the building. Clubs and societies, such as burial clubs, friendly societies, parish councils and even church meetings made it their headquarters. With so much going on in the tavern, it was inevitable that drink would be flowing freely, and there were many who would return to their homes considerably the worse for wear after an evening out. The working men's clubs in Runcorn which had Dr Grindrod as their medical officer were among those to use the tavern as their meeting place, and here he would have seen his chance to put forward proposals for change.

An obituary notice in the *Church of England Temperance Chronicle*, dated November 24,1883, records this stage in his career: "In 1830, Dr Grindrod was resident at Halton Castle, near Runcorn, Cheshire. As medical officer to some working men's clubs his attention was directed to the disorderly conduct of the members at their monthly and annual meetings through the drink imbibed at these gatherings, and his eyes were opened to the fact that intemperance was the working man's scourge. He designed certain alterations in the rules of the Friendly Society; but before he could carry them into effect he removed to Manchester, having accepted an appointment as medical officer to the Chorlton-upon-Medlock Dispensary." The obituary notice is correct in stating that before he could carry out the reforms he removed to Manchester, although he did not become medical officer to the dispensary but instead went into private practice. It is more likely that his proposals for reform were unacceptable to his clients, and having become a persona non grata in Runcorn he could have seen Manchester as more fertile soil for propagating his views.

On his return to Manchester Dr Grindrod set up his practice near St Luke's Church in Cheetham Hill Road, and later he moved to 3 and then 5 Ancoats Street. He was somewhat amused to find that at one of these addresses he had the Crown and Kettle only two doors away, and on the other side a beer shop and the Nelson Tavern. Certainly he was well positioned for pursuing his temperance work! While he was in Cheetham Hill Road he had his consulting rooms in a former chemist's shop, and this gave rise to a rumour that he was merely a druggist, a charge he was quick to deny.

Besides his involvement in a busy and successful practice, he found time to join actively in a number of societies that flourished in Manchester at that period. Welcomed as a colleague by many of his former teachers and medical friends, he was soon enrolled as a member of the Manchester Literary and Philosophical Society which was founded in 1781 by two members of the staff of the Manchester Royal Infirmary. Despite its name it had a strong bias towards medical and scientific interests, which is hardly surprising since John Dalton, who had been a member from 1794, became its president in 1817. In 1834 this society was succeeded by a new foundation, the Manchester Medical Society, with Dr John Hull as president. As Hon Physician to the Lying-in-Hospital, John Hull had made a name for himself as one of the early defenders of Caesarean operations, and he was also a keen and able botanist whose *British Flora* (1799) became a standard work on the subject. In 1838 Dr Grindrod's old friend James Bardsley took over the presidency, and it was he who, much to Dr Grindrod's pleasure, gave him an unsolicited testimonial on the occasion of his leaving Manchester. The ability to work closely with medical colleagues greatly helped Dr Grindrod in his subsequent career, and typical of this was the co-operation they gave him in his own researches. He cites one example of this in the paper on hydrophobia which he contributed to the second volume of *The Transactions of the Provincial Medical and Surgical Association* in 1836.

Another important interest for Dr Grindrod was the Manchester Statistical Society in which bankers and medical men played a particularly prominent part. Its first treasurer, Dr James P. Kay (later Sir James Kay-Shuttleworth) represented both occupations, since before qualifying as a doctor he had served an apprenticeship in a Manchester bank. His pamphlet *The Physical and Moral Conditions of the Working Classes Employed in the Cotton Manufacture in Manchester* ran into two editions in 1832, and in the following year he was active in the setting up of the society. Later he played a prominent part in the development of public education. The Manchester society was the first of the provincial societies concerned with collecting accurate statistics for the use of those concerned with social legislation and reform. Not only was Dr Grindrod closely involved with their relevance to the Manchester scene, but his interest in statistics underpinned a large number of his later writings. He also had links abroad as he was elected a Corresponding Member of the National Institute, Washington, and of the Statistical Society of France.

Apart from these activities and his day to day work as a general practitioner, Dr Grindrod's main contribution to life in Manchester was his espousal of the cause of temperance. Many local temperance societies already existed throughout the country, often connected with the churches and especially Nonconformist bodies such as the Quakers, Baptists and Methodists. There was also a London based national society, the British and Foreign Temperance Society, which had as its president the Bishop of London. It had branches in many other parts of the country and was particularly well supported in the northern counties. While many of these societies included members with teetotal principles, they were for the most part anti-spirit movements, with the stress on moderation rather than total abstinence. Because of this they found support in somewhat unexpected quarters. It was not at all unusual, for example, for millowners and other proprietors of businesses to chair temperance meetings. A sober disciplined work force was, after all, beneficial to industry, and the money that might have been squandered on drink could promote the sale of manufactured goods and so keep people in employment. As the Preston MP and teetotaller, Joseph Livesey, argued in 1833: "Nearly all the money spent at public houses ought to be, and if teetotalism prevailed, would be spent at your shops." Even more unexpected was the support of many brewers and owners of public houses. An anti-spirits movement could give the brewer an expanded market for his less intoxicating drinks, and it was certainly in the interests of the public house owner that his reputation should not suffer from drunken brawling on his premises.

Soon after his return to Manchester Dr Grindrod joined the Salford and Manchester Temperance Society which had been founded on the moderation principle. His main contribution to its activities at first was in the form of lectures, but he also wrote and edited a series of tracts that were published in 1835. In the same year he became president and used his influence to encourage the committee to take on far-sighted schemes. Aware that lectures and tracts fell far short of what was really needed, he made a number of proposals for the general welfare of members that would also help with future recruitment. In the view of P.T.Winskill, these measures "prove beyond doubt that he was one of the most advanced temperance reformers of the country at this early date."

Already the society had begun to establish coffee-rooms and eating houses in various parts of the town, and this innovation he believed should be developed, as an alternative to resorting to the public house and the beer and gin shops. But a much more extensive programme of social reform was now proposed, to include the following: reading rooms with books and periodicals (he is reputed as having half-emptied his library of books of general interest for this purpose); writing and reading schools for those who previously lacked any opportunity of education, and classes in subjects such as music and practical mechanics; lectures on subjects, other than temperance, connected with the interests of the working-classes; a general registry office to help members of the society find suitable employment; and rooms for friendly societies and sick clubs, so that meetings need not be held in public houses.

Among the societies actually set up by Dr Grindrod was one for children which was connected with St Paul's Church and was a branch of the Church of England Temperance Society. Known as the Juvenile Temperance Society, it held its meetings in the Manchester Mechanics Institute in Cooper Street, an educational foundation in which he had always taken the greatest interest. In later years when the temperance movement had an enormously successful children's society known as the Band of Hope, discussion arose as to the identity of its founder. The answer seems to be that while the actual name was given first to a society founded by Mr Carlile in Dublin in 1845, Dr Grindrod's conviction that the cause of temperance was best served by recruiting young people before they could develop a taste for alcohol led him by that time to have developed such societies all over the country.

While, unlike some convinced teetotallers, Dr Grindrod was willing to support the societies that stood for moderation, he was determined to promote the cause of total abstinence. Wine and beer might be less potent than spirits, but in his view it was too easy a step from moderation to excess, and therefore all strong drink should be discouraged. He himself took a pledge of total abstinence in 1832, and followed it up later with what was known as the longer pledge. The former was applicable only to the signatory's personal practice, while the latter required him also to abstain from offering drink to others. He explains this difference in a letter to the *Alliance News* (1881): "I administered not only the exclusive total abstinence principle, but the long pledge, which promised not merely total abstinence, but abstinence in relation to giving or offering it to others. It was also a life pledge." It was his belief that he was the first medical man in the country to sign the teetotal pledge.

His first venture into forming a total abstinence society was in 1834 at Miles Platting, a densely populated district of Manchester. Cottages arranged around a square near Riders Row became the scene of weekly meetings, and when they became overcrowded he moved into the open square. Two large tables were set up as a platform, and here throughout the summer Dr Grindrod argued his case, mainly from a medical angle. According to Winskill, this society was "the first general public and exclusively teetotal society in England." It was later absorbed into the New British and Foreign Society for the Suppression of Intemperance, which in 1839 became the New British and Foreign Temperance Society. Unlike the earlier B.F.T.S. this N.B.F.T.S. emphasised teetotalism.

At one of the Miles Platting meetings a Baptist minister, the Rev Frances Beardsall, who was to become a leading promoter of the temperance movement, signed the total abstinence pledge. His first move was to form in September 1834 an influential group known as the Oak Street Temperance Society. Although he himself favoured the teetotal position, this society was founded on the dual basis.

The following year was marked by a four day festival in which the Oak Street Society played host to temperance groups in other parts of Manchester and Lancashire towns such as Bolton and Preston. The proposal for a joint festival originated with Joseph Livesey, who was booked on this occasion to give his famous Malt Lecture, so named because much of it was an attempt to prove that popular confidence in the food value of beer and ale was a sad delusion. An audience of some 800 gathered to hear him, but unfortunately he was unable to attend. His lecture, however, was already in print and Mr Beardsall deputised for him by reading it to the assembled company. Throughout the festival there were well attended meetings in the Tabernacle, Stevenson Square, the first of which was addressed by Dr Grindrod, and these were followed each morning by open air rallies in the Square. Saturday was the high light of the occasion and was marked by a public procession. Headed by a brass band, some 1000 supporters paraded through the streets, with banners representing, among others, the Oak Street Temperance Sick and Burial Society. Such societies were founded as a means of discouraging people from belonging to similar welfare clubs that were in the practice of meeting in public houses.

It was either on this occasion or shortly afterwards that the movement enrolled a new convert, Mr John Cassell, who was to become one of its most influential workers. Born in Manchester in 1817, John Cassell was a carpenter by trade. Impressed by the arguments for total abstinence put forward by Dr Grindrod, he gave up his work as a carpenter and found employment as a travelling agent for the N.B.F.T.S. which involved addressing public meetings, distributing tracts and other such activities. He made a point of announcing his coming with a watchman's rattle, which he regarded as an appropriate method of warning against intemperance. Because he was a self-educated man he was a great believer in the value of the written word, and after his marriage to a lady of means he acquired a printing press and issued a large number of temperance tracts. Eventually he went into partnership with the already established printers, Messrs Petter and Galpin, and this was to become in due course the publishing firm of Cassell which still continues to-day.

As might be expected, promotion of total abstinence aroused much more antagonism than did the preaching of moderation. In August 1835, Mr J.Youil, landlord of the Hen and Chickens Hotel in Oldham Street and also brewer of a famous ale, called "tenpenny" because of its strength, staged an opposition. He organised a public meeting in Stevenson Square, which was close to his hotel and it attracted an audience of some ten to fifteen thousand. There was nothing particularly unusual about these numbers, and Dr Grindrod's lectures in the Square had probably already often drawn just such a crowd. Open air orators of every shade of opinion could expect to get a hearing in the Square. In the words of T.Swindells: "Innumerable have been the causes advocated from improvised platforms. Religious gatherings representing most phases of religious thought, temperance and social reform meetings, and mass meetings of Liberals, Conservatives, Socialists and Chartists have been held there. Perhaps the advocates of total abstinence have been the most persistent of the many speakers who have aired their eloquence there."[1] He goes on to mention Dr Grindrod specifically as one of the earliest and most determined advocates of this policy. Now it was the turn of the opposition and Mr Youil was a well known character.

Mr Youil's meeting purported to be a discussion, and as representative of the teetotal point of view Dr Grindrod was given a place on the platform. Although an extremely able lecturer with a good command of his subject, Mr Youil took the precaution of packing the meeting with his own supporters, including having twenty to thirty publicans and wine merchants also on the platform. Moreover he was an adept in more devious ways of gaining popularity and organised a distribution of thousands of leaflets supporting his case. These were illustrated with caricatures representing the doctor on the back of a crocodile, and in contrast Milo the champion of drink carrying an ox on his back as symbol of his great strength. He was also not above descending to personal remarks to the detriment of his adversary: "Look at him! Does he look as if he had ever indulged in port, hock, sherry, turtle, venison, turkey, or even oyster sauce? No; more likely soupe maigre. Has he sparks of wit, humour, or good nature about him? He not only envies us our ale, but would even break our pipes! Surely he is not angry with us because every whiff we take increases the revenue."[2]. The lecture was later published with the title *Teetotalism Calmly Investigated*.

Dr Grindrod recognised that in Mr Youil he had a formidable opponent. His own immediate comment on the lecture was: "it was a very clever one and exhibited much ability and research." He was aware however that the climate of the meeting was not one in which rational discussion could be attempted, and accordingly he proposed presenting his case in a series of lectures.

On three successive evenings he gave his considered reply to Mr Youil at vast indoor gatherings in the Tabernacle, Stevenson Square. He claimed that "at the conclusion of the third lecture a vote, a unanimous vote, was passed in support of teetotalism." One suspects that here too the meeting was packed with known supporters, and if any of the listeners had thought of voting otherwise they had either seized an opportunity to absent themselves, or if still present lacked the courage to stand against the popular line.

The strain of these sessions proved too much for Dr Grindrod's health. In his own words: "My individual exertions on three successive evenings to a crowded audience of at least 3000 persons, and from two to three hours each evening, induced complete exhaustion and confinement to my bed for several days, during which my old and warm friend Sir James Bardsley was my medical attendant."

Attracting big crowds did not always have such a satisfactory outcome. Only five months later, on January 26,1836, a crowded temperance meeting took place in a recently erected chapel in Oldham Street. The floor gave way, and as a result two persons were killed and sixty to seventy injured. Dr Grindrod, who was at the time exhausted and ill with overwork, was not among those present, but when news of the accident reached him he was immediately on the scene giving what help he could to the victims. Some in the crowd voiced their views that no good would come of temperance, while one was even heard to say: "I only wish that Grindrod was under the ruins." But many of the sufferers voiced opposing views, as for example, a woman who remarked to Dr Stanley, Rector of Alderley (who later became Bishop of Norwich): "Sir, if I knew I should suffer ten times as much, I could endure it all for the great benefits I have received from the temperance cause." Dr Stanley himself was so impressed with Dr Grindrod's arguments in favour of teetotalism as well as with the uncomplaining behaviour of so many of these sufferers that he decided to become an abstainer himself. Later his doctor prevailed upon him to accept alcohol for medical use, but he remained a firm supporter of the movement. The meeting between Dr Stanley and Dr Grindrod marked the beginning of a long friendship, and some years later Dr Stanley, who by then was President of the Linnaean Society, put his friend forward as a Fellow of the Society. He also encouraged him to seek ordination.

One of the newspaper reporters who arrived at the scene of the accident was more impressed with Dr Grindrod's generosity than with his temperance views. The fact that a doctor might give his services entirely free seems to have amazed him. He recorded: "Dr Grindrod, in his medical capacity, without fee or reward, attended the whole of the sufferers, supplying them with medicine and other aid, and also obtained liberal subscriptions on behalf of the distressed."

Despite the strength of his convictions, which extended beyond temperance to other issues such as his evangelical faith, Dr Grindrod could be relied on to give a fair hearing to opposing views. An interesting example of this was his chairmanship of a public discussion on the principles of Owenism and Christianity, with Robert Owen representing the former and the Rev J.H.R.Roebuck the latter. Robert Owen was a keen reformer whose approach to the problems of industrialisation was on humanist and co-operative lines. His humanist convictions left no room for appeals to Christian values as a mainspring of conduct, and this brought him often into conflict with Christian reformers. *The Templar* (April 23, 1874) describes this occasion: "The followers of Owen were very numerous in

Mrs. Mary Whiteley Grindrod

Manchester – so potential as to be enabled to erect a large hall in the centre of the City. The followers of Owen were avowed infidels, Dr Grindrod was an active member of the Evangelical Church of England . . . The disputants selected were Robert Owen and the Rev J.H.Roebuck. Both parties united in requesting Dr Grindrod to take the chair, having confidence in his impartial rule. He did so, an assent being given that the proceeds of charge for admission should be devoted to the cause of Temperance, and nearly £100 was added to the funds of the Society."

If there were any truth in Mr Youil's description of Dr Grindrod, other than the implication that he lacked the bonhomie and corpulent figure of a Friar Tuck, one might wonder whether he would have difficulty finding a congenial partner. But perhaps Mr Winskill's description may have been nearer the truth: "At the commencement of the temperance movement Dr Grindrod was young, active, intelligent, studious, zealous, and occupying a good social position . . .". At the age of twenty-five he found the ideal partner. This was Mary Whiteley Hull,[3] only daughter of John and Mary Whiteley Hull, whom he married in the Collegiate Church (later Manchester Cathedral) on August 30, 1837. She was two years older than her husband, and, sadly for a man who loved children, it was some years before their son was born. A teetotaller before her marriage, she had the satisfaction of being able to give strong support to her husband's work and was to earn for herself a distinguished place in the annals of the temperance movement.

5

The Power of the Pen

In 1838 an event occurred which was to have a far-reaching influence on Dr Grindrod's subsequent career. The New British and Foreign Temperance Society offered a prize of 100 sovereigns for the best essay on *The Benefits of Total Abstinence from all Intoxicating Drinks*. During his active work for the temperance cause Dr Grindrod had given much attention to studying the subject and keeping abreast with publications, especially those written from a medical angle. He was therefore well equipped to enter the contest, and submitted a work entitled *Bacchus*. He was awarded the prize on the recommendation of three adjudicators: the Rev Theodore Drury, Rector of Keighley; the Rev J.H.Hinton; and Mr J.E.Howard. Mr Drury was already well known, not only in the temperance movement but also for his activities in defence of workers through the regulation of factory hours.

The term essay gives a wrong impression, for *Bacchus* was in fact a monumental work of some 350,000 words. It was first published in 1839 with a print run of 10,000 copies. Almost simultaneously a large edition appeared in the United States, edited by Dr Charles A. Lee, Professor of Medicine at Union College, New York. In 1851 a second edition, with some revision, was issued by Simpkins Marshall & Co in London. Its 420 pages, each divided into two columns and with very small print, do not make for easy reading. The author himself was aware of this, and a later encounter with the distinguished surgeon Sir James Simpson of Edinburgh afforded him some amusement as well as gratification. "What only book do you think I took with me to read in my leisure moments on my wedding tour?" asked the latter. On receiving no reply, he added, "*Bacchus*"!

The book begins with a survey of the history of intemperance, from Bible times through the classical era and then throughout the world to the present time. In this section the author shows particularly the part religious practices, even those of Christianity, have played in encouraging Bacchanalian excesses. He quotes the denunciation of

Cyprian, the third century Bishop of Carthage: "Drunkenness is so common with us in Africa that it scarce passes for a crime. And do we not see Christians forcing one another to get drunk to celebrate the memory of the martyrs." But throughout the centuries and even today, he notes, such customs as wakes and Whitsun revels are no less harmful. He then enlarges on the various causes of alcoholism. He quotes from the many poets who like Robert Burns have claimed drink as their inspiration. He also enumerates some of the social causes such as the lack of opportunity for developing other forms of enjoyment, and the constant bombardment of society with drink on such occasions as auctions, feasts commemorating victory in war and politics, and the meetings of clubs and friendly societies in public houses; the list is formidable.

Because his special interest is in the medical aspect, he gives much attention to attacking the delusion that alcoholic drink is a source of strength. Perhaps here he is indebted to Livesey's Malt Lectures as well as his own researches. "The plodding traveller," he writes, "considers alcohol as the indispensable companion of his journeys; the labouring man views it as his cheering friend during unceasing toil and exertion; and the student, he of the midnight oil, has recourse to its exhilarating influence during moments of mental depression and physical debility." Such belief in its strength-giving properties, he points out, is fostered by the names by which it is advertised: elixir vitae, eau de vie, strong lusty London beer, etc. The defenders of moderate drinking have, in his view, no case. Any form of strong drink has the physical effect of fostering an urge for more: "each act of indulgence but strengthens the fetters which bind the unhappy victim;" and he points out that the immediate experience of exhilaration only leads to depression and debility. On this point he quotes Dr J. Baxter of New York and other New York medical practitioners who maintained that improper diet and physical exhaustion, because of weather and excessive labour, created a need for liquor; but in fact "the remedy leads to evils incomparably worse than the disease." While admitting that medical men differed, he nevertheless claims that habitual use of strong drink was generally condemned. He notes too that tobacco and opium stimulate a need for drink, and comments that the former should be discouraged while the latter should perhaps be added to the temperance pledge. He then details the many proprietary medicines which included alcohol in their composition and quotes a number of leading doctors, particularly in the USA, who condemned their use. The conviction that physical exertion and work in abnormally hot or cold climates required the use of liquor is also dismissed as a fallacy, and he expresses his belief that diseases of the liver in tropical countries are due not to the climate but to the drinking habits of the victims. In his view, "the strong drink delusion has been one of the most fallacious, as well as deep-rooted and fatal, that ever took possession of the human mind."

A considerable section of the book takes up the theme of moderate drinking. He had for long been moving in the direction of regarding moderation as a snare rather than a blessing, since those who believed they could take drink in moderation so easily found themselves bewitched into pursuing the downward path into excess. He quotes the example of Hannah More urging Dr Johnson to take a little wine, and his reply: "I can't take a little, child; therefore I never touch it. Abstinence is as easy to me as temperance would be difficult." Even moderate drinking, Dr Grindrod maintains, could have a detrimental effect in such matters as temper and social intercourse, speech, moral powers, intellectual faculties, judgment, memory and many others. As one of many illustrations of its effect on social intercourse he quotes Byron's comments on Sheridan at a party when wine was circulated: "First silent, then talking, then argumentative, then disputatious, then unintelligible, then inarticulate, and then drunk."

At this point the book makes extensive use of evidence from the 1834 Buckingham Report, so-called because it owed its origin to the work of Mr J.S.Buckingham, MP for Sheffield, who had persuaded Parliament to hold an enquiry into drunkenness, and had furnished the committee with an enormous amount of material from his own researches in this country and America. According to the *Metropolitan Temperance Intelligencer* (February 25, 1843) this report long remained "the Text Book of every teetotal advocate, the source whence he drew his richest facts, his most important arguments." What gave it special value was its emphasis on statistical evidence to support its statements, and much of this is incorporated into *Bacchus*.

A major section of the book is devoted to the physical damage to the human system caused by alcohol. As a doctor it was the medical aspect of the subject that most interested him. After dismissing the claim that alcohol is a food, he proceeds to denounce it as a poison, both in its nature and operation. He enlarges on its deleterious effects on the various parts of the body and particularly on the digestive system. Its irritating effects he compares to putting pepper or vinegar in the eye, and he quotes in detail a recent study of the damage to an open stomach wound reported by an American physician Dr Beaumont, whose work had made a great stir in the medical world. Careful examination of his patient had led Dr Beaumont to the conclusion that "the free use of ardent spirits, wines, beer, or any intoxicating liquor, when continued for some days, has invariably produced these morbid changes."

Many examples are also given of the part played by alcohol in cholera epidemics. Here he was able to draw on his own medical experience, and he backed it up by quoting a recent report in the *Morning Herald* which alleged that "in some towns the drunkards are all dead." Damage to the brain and nervous system is also dealt with, and statistical tables are brought in to show the percentage of people admitted to lunatic asylums as a result of drink in towns such as Glasgow, Edinburgh, Aberdeen, Wakefield, etc. Besides leading to madness, it was also responsible for contributing to illnesses and conditions such as palsy, epilepsy, apoplexy and delirium tremens.

A section of the book outlines the history of the processes of distillation and fermentation, and makes a detailed examination of the nature and chemical properties of various types of drink. Much of this information was probably gathered in response to opposition from publicans such as Mr Youil, who were incensed by what they saw as his attempts to undermine their means of livelihood. He was careful to draw a distinction between wine that was produced mainly by a process of fermentation and the much more potent types of drink, such as spirits and fortified wines of which port was particularly popular. While both in his view came into the category of poison, the latter group was much more deadly, and he was insistent that much that passed for wine in this country was in fact contaminated by many other additives.

The book ends with a study of the measures employed down the ages and in various countries to combat intemperance. Laws he dismisses as mainly inefficient. Educational institutions had played a part, but had concentrated too much on intellectual instruction and not enough attention had been given to moral and religious training. More should have been done to create an awareness of the need to improve working conditions and social welfare. The medical profession had failed people by recommending alcohol as a medicine, and it is important that this practice should be abandoned. The temperance societies had been making an important contribution in educating people to understand the true nature of this social evil, but they needed to concentrate on promoting total abstinence as the only safe and effective cure for intemperance.

An outline of the range of topics dealt with in *Bacchus* in no way does it justice. The wealth of illustrative material drawn from his own extensive reading and professional experience is a marked feature of the book and much of it makes fascinating reading. Perhaps a more selective approach would have enhanced the impact of its message as well as improving its literary quality, but it is a serious attempt to present the case for total abstinence on the basis of science and rationality, rather than appealing to the emotions in the style of so much temperance literature.

What was said of the Buckingham Report is still more true of *Bacchus*. For many years it remained the Bible of the temperance worker, and Dr Grindrod's reputation as an authority on the subject was second to none. Writing in 1877, John Guthrie in his book *Temperance Physiology* sums up what it meant to the early temperance workers: "Dr Grindrod's singularly learned and exhaustive prize essay *Bacchus* produced a profound impression, and still stands unsurpassed as a storehouse of miscellaneous temperance argument and illustration, which, as might be expected, is especially rich and copious on the chemical and physiological aspects of the question . . . In this essay, whatever had been previously done in the way of alcoholic investigation is duly chronicled and expounded with much original elucidation by the author himself; and consequently, considering the vast strides that have lately been made in the determination of the true character and workings of alcohol, it is interesting to note the comparative maturity of those earlier views, and to what extent they anticipated more recent results."[1]

An almost immediate result of the publication of *Bacchus* was that Dr Grindrod received an honorary LLD from Union College, New York; and subsequently, in 1842, on the strength of his submission of *Bacchus* and a dissertation on *Disease Without Sensation*, the University of Erlangen awarded him the degree of MD.

*   *   *

On a very different scale from *Bacchus* were the two pamphlets published a few years later on the subject of working conditions in Manchester and other parts of the country. Although comparatively short they were considered of sufficient significance to have been reprinted in New York in 1972 from copies in the possession of Harvard's Graduate School of Business Administration. *The Wrongs of Our Youth; An Essay on the Evils of the Late-Hour System* was originally published in 1843. It exposed the unsatisfactory conditions of employment in such areas as domestic work, dressmaking, metal and earthenware manufacturing, paper-making, weaving, printing, and subordinate jobs in shops, warehouses and offices. *The Slaves of the Needle; An Exposure of the Distressed Condition, Moral and Physical, of Dress-Makers, Milliners, Embroiderers, Slop-Workers etc.* followed in 1844.

The Wrongs of Our Youth was appropriately dedicated to Lord Ashley in recognition of his work for the improvement of factory conditions, which was to lead to the passing of the Ten Hours Bill in

1847. The dedication notes that his "philanthropic exertions on behalf of suffering humanity, peculiarly entitle him to the honourable distinction of The Friend of the Poor". Much of the material in these two pamphlets is derived from evidence given in Parliamentary reports.

Apart from the fact that the first pamphlet dealt primarily with young people and the latter with women of all ages, the two had much in common. Unlike some propagandists of the period Dr Grindrod was not concerned with movements directed towards encouraging working people to improve their lot by organizing themselves into any form of Trade Union. His approach was essentially an effort to arouse the social conscience of employers and ordinary members of the public. It was also based on Christian principles, and was underpinned by the conviction that if Christians and other persons of goodwill were made aware of the working conditions of the labouring classes they would be moved to support change. *The Slaves of the Needle* is specifically addressed to the "Ladies of Great Britain and Ireland," in the hope that "it will excite those kind and generous feelings which they have ever evinced in the cause of suffering humanity, and lead to the total extinction of a system as utterly repugnant to Christian principles as it is cruel and unnecessary."

Because of his own experience in general practice the medical aspect is paramount, just as it was in his temperance activities. Bad conditions at work took their toll on the health of his patients, and he collects material from his own experience in Manchester as well as from other well-known medical men to illustrate the various points of his thesis. Long hours of work were particularly to blame. Not only did these militate against a normal social life and any chance of educational advancement, but he saw them as a direct cause of stunted physical growth and sickness. Moreover the appalling physical conditions in which the work was done served to acerbate the problem. Evidence supplied by physicians was remarkably unanimous with regard to the sufferings of their patients, although the conditions varied according to the type of work in which they were employed. Stunted growth, weight loss, stomach complaints, gynaecological problems, bronchial and pulmonary troubles leading often to phthisis and an early death, were common among many of those employed for long hours in poorly ventilated rooms and perhaps subjected to fumes from the gas lighting or inhaling of dust. In some workrooms or in the workers' homes if they were employed in piece work, only candles were available, and the damage to eyes from fine needlework was widespread. This frequently led to blindness. Typical evidence from a medical practitioner is quoted: "The very early age at which children begin to work, the sedentary nature of the occupation, the constrained and stooping position, and the crowded state of the workrooms lead to serious constitutional debility and disease. These children are particularly subject to various scrofulous affections: diseases of the eye, especially strumous inflammation, are common; also swelling of the joints, etc." In some cases up to 40 children were at work for some thirteen hours in rooms that were described as "very confined and ill-ventilated."

Dr Grindrod himself was particularly concerned with the distortion to the spine suffered by sedentary workers, especially sempstresses. He details the structure of the spine, showing with appropriate illustrations, how it is affected by posture, and notes that such women have increased susceptibility to such damage because of their "feeble and debilitated frame." In evidence he quotes from a letter he had received from a Dr Charles Clay who had a practice in Piccadilly, Manchester. This doctor had taken careful note from his own experience, possibly in the first instance to supply evidence for the Manchester Statistical Society which at that time was conducting a survey of conditions in industry. He writes: "I have by me notes of about 600 cases of milliners and dressmakers of a dependent nature, 150 of which had distorted spines to a very great extent, and fifty more of less extent; 140 had emaciated constitutions with severe coughs, many of these confirmed phthisis; 40 more with coughs less severe; 65 suffering from other diseases, more particularly applicable to females of sedentary employments, and likely to terminate fatally... I do not wonder at this, from the knowledge of one fact. Some years ago, I knew of seven girls confined from 5 or 6 o'clock in the morning to 10, 11, and sometimes 12 at night, in a room of 3¼ yards square, in which was a fire, and at night two strong gas lights, burning constantly. The seven girls were all unhealthy; four had crooked spines; not one without a cough. Two were originally delicate; but five came out of the country, in the bloom of health, and had not been at the trade two years."

The conditions of work referred to by Dr Clay were in fact better than those experienced by many of these workers. Poor food and inadequate breaks in which to eat it were usual, and the hours far exceeded the 7 or 8 am to 11 pm that was considered acceptable. An example is given of a woman who stated that for 3 months successively "she had never more than four hours' rest, regularly going to bed between twelve and one, and getting up at four in the morning. On the occasion of the general mourning for his Majesty William IV, witness worked without going to bed from four o'clock on Thursday morning, till half past ten on Sunday morning; during this time witness did not sleep at all: of this she is certain. In order to keep awake, she stood nearly the whole of Friday, Saturday, and Saturday night only sitting down for half an hour for rest." Such conditions were movingly pictured in Thomas Hood's famous "Song of the Shirt" which Dr Grindrod quotes in full, introducing it with the note that "the following admirable verses, said to be the composition of Thomas Hood, were lately published in one of our popular periodicals." Perhaps its publication had influenced him in his own writing on the subject.

Dr Grindrod noted that the periods of serious overwork were commonly in connexion with weddings, funerals, and the fashionable season, because clothes were then required at short notice. While he was aware that some exceptions might have to be made for funerals, he emphasised that employers could improve the situation by a willingness to take on extra hands. Lady customers should however recognise that they had it in their power to make life easier for the workers: "The evidence of witnesses shows, that much mischief results from the inconsiderateness of ladies, whose orders for dresses are not infrequently, but unnecessarily delayed until the last possible moment. Weddings are not concluded in a day, nor, as a general rule, is the period arranged for interment, so early as to render night work unavoidable. Few balls, indeed, or other festive occasions, take place without sufficient previous intimation. No excuse, therefore, remains for an unnecessary delay in orders for dress." His appeal therefore was to the customers, who, he believed, would act in the interests of these women, if made aware of their conditions of employment: "Each act of procrastination but adds one more pang of sorrow to the oppressed and unprotected slave of the needle. The bride, in her gayous adornments, with features redolent of present joy, and future hopes, would scarcely maintain the same unmingled feelings of pleasure and delight, if she was conscious that an aching head, and exhausted frame, and a depressed and broken spirit, had entered into the production of her bridal costume."

But poor pay was no less responsible for the sufferings of the work force, and while resident employees might be inadequately recompensed, those who took in sewing and the women inmates of the workhouses were even more poorly paid. Consequently many who tried to support themselves in this way were being drawn into prostitution. Typical payments are quoted: "Not long ago, two daughters of a deceased major in the army, through adverse circumstances, were obliged to seek a precarious support by the aid of the needle . . . On after investigation it was found that, for every Shirt furnished to the tradesman, they received THREE-HALFPENCE; and by incessant labour, at the utmost stretch of speed, for ten hours, the unfortunate lady was enabled to earn FOURPENCE-HALFPENNY. Out of this paltry sum she had to provide herself with needles, thread, the candlelight necessary for her employment, in addition to food and clothing and rent."

Dr Grindrod was fully aware that there was no easy solution to this problem, but he was convinced that much could be achieved by making known the facts of the case. This could lead to such measures as ladies making known to employers their determination to withhold their patronage from those unwilling to improve conditions, and also themselves refraining from "the pernicious practice of cheapening goods." Moreover some depots for the sale of goods could be set up where the workers could be given fair payment and a guarantee of regular employment.

The topics dealt with in these pamphlets were among those in which Dr Grindrod was to have a continuing interest. That he should have been actively involved at this particular time was only natural as he might hope to have some influence on public opinion in the years when Parliament was engaged on these questions. In later years when he became the proprietor of *The Malvern Advertiser* he showed the same determination to back up the reformers, by devoting many of his editorials to similar subjects of social concern.

6

Temperance Travels: Touring the North

The early 1840s, which saw the publication of his pamphlets on working conditions, was a period of some uncertainty for Dr Grindrod. He was well-established in his Manchester practice and was highly regarded by the local medical fraternity. The publication of *Bacchus*, together with his active promotion of temperance, gained him a reputation not only in the immediate neighbourhood, but much further afield among the many individuals and societies that were promoting the cause throughout the British Isles and overseas. This work, however, was absorbing so much time and energy that he began to wonder whether it was possible to do justice both to it and to his medical practice.

Motivated strongly by the desire to help people to a better life, he was also turning over in his mind the encouragement given to him by both Bishop Sumner and Bishop Stanley to seek ordination in the Anglican Church. Religion had always been important to him, and although he was disappointed that support for total abstinence came more from the Baptists and members of other Free Churches than from Anglicans, he recognised that many reformed drunkards attributed their change of life to their religious faith. But besides giving him a new sphere of influence, he could see the practical advantage of having greater freedom from commitments as a clergyman than as a doctor. More time, therefore, could be given to the work of temperance reform. He refers to this in a lecture in Doncaster in 1845, which was reported in the *Doncaster Gazette* (15 & 22 August). "His reasons for leaving the medical profession were solely upon the grounds that he could not continue to exercise his philanthropic calling in that capacity, while by entering the church he would have more leisure to devote amongst his brethren in the promotion of temperance." But the call to a more ambitious programme of temperance work was also presenting itself. His success in Manchester had been so great that he began to envisage the possibility of spreading the gospel of teetotalism to a much wider public, and in this he had the encouragement of many of his friends. Many leaders of the movement were already at work in this field, but often they were reformed drunkards with only limited education, whose message was primarily emotional in character. He appreciated their work, but felt that there was a need for a professional medical man to present the case to an educated public who might yield to persuasion if the approach were based on scientific argument and presented in a calm and reasoned way. This was an undertaking which he now saw as a challenge. He had already proved himself as a lecturer capable of holding the attention of vast audiences. He had private means, and his wife, who was in sympathy with his work, was in a similar position. Moreover there was as yet no sign of children and therefore neither partner felt fettered by home ties.

Before coming to a final decision about ordination he gave up his practice and committed himself to a six months' tour of some northern towns and cities under the auspices of the temperance societies in each place. In the event the tour proved so successful that the thought of ordination was put aside, and he embarked on what was to become a six and a half year mission throughout the length and breadth of England. He called it his medical temperance mission, and he became known in temperance circles as "the great medical apostle of temperance," a title given to him first in Burnley.

It was natural that Dr Grindrod should begin his lecturing tour on territory close to home. His first engagement was in Liverpool. Although the programme here was much less ambitious than on subsequent occasions, it set the pattern for future developments. His lectures on February 5 and 6, 1844, under the presidency of Mr Lawrence Heyworth, were held in The Portico, Newington. Mr Heyworth, a tireless worker for the various Liverpool societies and himself a total abstainer, was wholly sympathetic to Dr Grindrod's ideals, and he and his committee were concerned that the lectures should be attended by the type of person who could benefit from this educational approach. They also saw to it that publicity was given by the press, and the *Liverpool Courier* both advertised and reported the lectures at some length.

Two well known medical practitioners in Liverpool were so impressed with the quality of his lectures that they produced an unsolicited testimonial, recommending that temperance societies throughout the country should invite him for a visit. It read as follows: "We, the undersigned, members of the medical profession in Liverpool, feel anxious that every society in the kingdom should, without delay, engage Dr Grindrod to deliver his lectures on the 'Physiological Influence of Alcohol on the Human Frame'. We were so deeply impressed with the conviction of the great importance and high value of his lectures, that we advise, yea, urge, all societies to avail themselves of his services, and to make extraordinary exertions to obtain large congregations, such as would be in character with the magnitude of his display, and the richness, variety, and convincing demonstration of his addresses. We would suggest to all societies which may engage him, the propriety of forming a picture-gallery with his drawings. A great sensation was produced on those who had the pleasure of hearing the lectures. The drawings are beautiful works of art on a magnificent scale and accurate representations of the diseased appearances of the various organs of the human frame, mainly produced by intoxicating beverages, and so numerous as to cover the walls of a large hall. We think that special invitations should be sent to every medical gentleman in each locality where he may lecture, requesting them to visit this unparalleled gallery of pathological drawings. We wish him great success in his philanthropic enterprise . . . John B. Burrows, Thomas Eden, Liverpool, February 13,1844."[1]

The pathological drawings referred to in the testimonial were to prove an effective means of getting his message across, and the macabre nature of many of them kept children spellbound. To these drawings were added mechanical models and other objects which enabled him to demonstrate experimentally some of his points. No expense was spared in acquiring these valuable aids. P.T. Winskill describes those used in Liverpool: "He made great preparations for this campaign, having had a skilled artist employed for some months in the preparation of an extensive series of coloured diagrams exhibiting the healthy condition of the entire human organs, with corresponding ones of organs exhibiting diseased conditions induced by alcoholic indulgence. These included drawings of the stomach, liver, heart, lungs, brain, kidneys and bowels. In addition to these he had a number of models to illustrate the action of the heart and respiration, exhibiting the movements of these organs by mechanical contrivances; a series of bottles filled with drugs used in adulteration, and also apparatus for distillation and for exhibiting the quantity of spirit contained in various alcoholic drinks." At a later stage in his progress throughout the country he added further exhibits of an even more lurid character. A syllabus of his lectures includes the information that "The Doctor also illustrates his subject by busts of five idiots, the successive children of the same drunken parents, who when sober had a child born to them with the perfect possession of all its faculties. He has also the busts of other children, and children preserved in spirits (before birth) of both drunken and sober parents."[2]

Following the auspicious beginning in Liverpool, Dr Grindrod accepted invitations in the next few months to a number of northern towns and cities. These included some very close to home: Knutsford, Runcorn and Warrington. He also covered a wide area in Yorkshire, which included Bradford, Halifax, Huddersfield, Leeds, Leyburn, Scarborough, Whitby and York. Reports on these visits suggest that the teaching aids were still making a great impression, and a correspondent to *The National Temperance Magazine* (1844 vol.1), who had attended the York lectures, suggested that fear might persuade more effectively than love: "*Fear* being a principle which *does* operate upon men, whilst *love*, which ought to be as unlimited in its influence, we know, by woeful experience, cannot be generally awakened."

A report in the same magazine urges that "all friends of the cause should arrange for these lectures to be given in their area," and goes into the question of meeting the cost of such an undertaking. It explains that while the Doctor preferred not even to accept a nominal fee for his services, he approved of the principle that all expenses should be met locally. While a charge for entrance to the meetings would help towards this, besides acting as a deterrent to the casual troublemaker, there needed to be a guarantee fund to meet any possible shortfall. The report continues: "The plan recommended is for committees to make an active personal canvass, calling the attention of clergymen, dissenting ministers, medical men, and other persons of influence: and thus securing a guarantee fund to indemnify the committee against loss. The Doctor desires that in every instance the lectures should pay themselves, which may be accomplished when proper means are used."

That expenses did sometimes prove a problem is indicated by a letter in the same magazine from a Jos Spence who had attended Dr Grindrod's York lectures. The sessions here were held in the Concert Room with an audience of 500 to 600. At the conclusion of the third lecture a collection was taken to meet a deficiency in the funds. It came to about £13, which proved sufficient to cover the £5 rental as well as allowing free admission for a fourth night when Dr Grindrod was able to deal with some of the questions that had arisen earlier. It was natural that some of the smaller places he visited would have more financial problems than would be experienced in the large industrial towns where 1000 or more might be present at a lecture.

Dr Grindrod was, however, not so much concerned with attracting large crowds as with finding opportunities to bring the message home to people of influence, especially doctors and clergy. The local temperance committees made a point of encouraging such people to occupy the platform or attend as members of the audience. P.T.Winskill comments on this aspect of his work: "What Mr Joseph Livesey did amongst the masses with his 'Malt Lecture,' and his able refutation of the 'Great Delusion,' Dr Grindrod with his scientific lectures accomplished among the clergy, medical men, and others in the higher circles of society. His lectures were scientific in their character, and excited the attention and attendance of thousands of clergymen, students, men of education and social position. The chairman at each lecture was almost in every instance a clergyman or physician." Medical men in particular were not easily converted to the cause if they already held opposing views and their presence often led to lively discussions. These could vary from friendly debate to acrimonious argument. Winskill records one of the more friendly contretemps which took place at Whitby on this first leg of Dr Grindrod's tour: "On the 23rd July, 1844, a discussion took place in the Temperance Hall, Whitby, Yorkshire, between Dr Grindrod and Mr Taylorson, surgeon. Mr R.Wilson presided, and the debate was conducted on both sides with much energy. At the conclusion a vote was taken, when the resolution in favour of teetotalism was carried with but one dissentient, and that one proposed a vote of thanks to the lecturer." This satisfactory outcome may not have been entirely due to Dr Grindrod's persuasive powers, for the organisers usually took care to pack the meetings with temperance supporters.

7

Temperance Travels: A Busy Schedule

At the end of the six months' trial period, when Dr Grindrod made his decision to go ahead with full-time temperance work, invitations to various parts of the country came thick and fast. Among so many it was not easy to select, but with the help of his wife he was able to plan a reasonable plan of campaign.

Mary Grindrod's part in her husband's medical mission should not be overlooked. The actual lecturing and all that was involved in personal contacts with both supporters and opponents made considerable demands on a man who was so emotionally involved in his work. In relating how he refused payment for his services, he mentions this problem of physical exhaustion: "On several occasions purses of gold were offered to me by way of help in my progress, and as a means of giving me occasional and needful rest. At times I was compelled, from absolute exhaustion, to cease active labour; and more than once my physical condition warned me that life itself was in danger. In every case I refused personal or private gifts, and received only the sum of money agreed to by each Committee, which did not, year by year, more than amount to the payment of expenses. This determination gave me a ready answer to malevolent reports circulated by unscrupulous opponents."[1] If it were not that his wife organised all the day to day practicalities and supported him on the pastoral side of his work, it is questionable whether the undertaking would have been so successful.

He was himself acutely aware of how much he owed to her unfailing support. In his own words: "As secretary, she conducted my large correspondence; and to her judgment and prudence I owe much of my success. This warm co-operation lightened my labours. The constant companionship of one who sympathised with and actively promoted my work did much, very much, to lighten the sometimes depressing circumstances to which I was subject. I must not, also, overlook the influence she exercised in association with individuals of her own sex, with whom we daily came in contact. Not merely did she meet their fears and objections with judicious statements, but invariably appealed to her own personal and encouraging experience. I could say more in her praise – I will not say more. The blessing of God attended our mutual exertions, and I cannot dissociate my own labours from one to whose sound judgment I owe so much, and whose sympathy and encouragement so largely strengthened my exertions."

This tribute from her husband is endorsed by P.T.Winskill who includes her in his record of the heroines of the temperance movement: "Honour is due to Mrs Grindrod for the invaluable aid and encouragement she gave her husband during the whole of his arduous labours. She was his amanuensis, travelling companion, counsellor, and friend; sacrificing home and all its comforts, enduring hardship and fatigue, she travelled some thousands of miles to assist her husband in his great work. In all his public efforts she was an efficient helpmeet, an amiable, earnest, self-sacrificing, heroic worker." It is good to know that her contribution was recognised from time to time in the places they visited. In Macclesfield, for example, where two free lectures were given to women only, each lecture attracting an audience of about two thousand, she was presented with a white satin dress, an appropriate gift for this centre of the silk trade. Leamington too showed its appreciation; in this case the gift of a silver teapot, perhaps in recognition of her own warm hospitality to her husband's clients.

Organising the travelling must have been a nightmare. Not only did they need to transport themselves, but there was also the unwieldy baggage that they had to take with them everywhere. Rail travel would be possible in some cases as by this time there was a skeleton network connecting many of the main cities and towns, but the very slow and uncomfortable stagecoach would often have to be used. Where neither of these was available plans for private transport would need to be organised. Some personal reminiscences of these hardships are recorded in the *British Temperance Advocate* in 1883: "My personal experience was a severe one. My lectures were chiefly delivered in the winter, and I commonly had to journey by the coach, and on the outside too – partly on the ground of economy, and partly because I could not bear the confinement and closeness of the inside. In numerous cases I hired a van or light carriage – large enough to convey my extensive luggage – with chairs or seats arranged on boxes for myself and wife. We often travelled in this primitive style for hundreds of miles – presenting not a very dignified aspect, but caring little so that our mission was successful. Frequently have we arrived at our journey's end saturated with the rain, or almost frozen with cold. These however were conditions to which we were often subjected."[2]

1845, the first full year of the tour, was exceptionally busy. In the spring, most of the visits were in Nottinghamshire and Lincolnshire. These included Bingham and Newham in Nottinghamshire; and Grantham, Lincoln, Boston and Spalding in Lincolnshire. The visit to Spalding presented him with an interesting problem. Temperance work was already well established in the area, but a local physician, Dr Morris, had undermined its influence by claiming that total abstinence was doing more harm than good. In particular, he alleged that "the mortality from typhus was greater among teetotallers . . . they appear to have no stamina left, and the shock is too much for the system to bear; they suffer also from malaria." Widespread publicity was given to his views in the *Provincial Medical Journal* and the press generally. Not surprisingly, Dr Grindrod took up the challenge, and after careful investigation he invited Dr Morris to attend a public debate on the subject.

Although the meeting was to be chaired by one of Dr Morris's personal friends who was not a pledged teetotaller, Dr Morris refused to accept the challenge. However, such was the public interest, that the meeting went ahead on April 6, 1845 in the Assembly Room, Spalding, a building designed to hold about eight hundred. When well over this number were demanding entry, it was deemed necessary to prop up the floor with artificial supports, a move perhaps prompted by Dr Grindrod's sad experience of the Manchester disaster. In refutation of Dr Morris's claims, Dr Grindrod produced evidence from a number of doctors in the Fen district, and backed this up with detailed statistics to prove his point. These listed all the teetotallers in the immediate area, giving names and periods of abstinence from alcohol, and the number of deaths from fever and malaria. P.T.Winskill notes: "The deaths from fevers of every description were 27 and only one of malaria." He then adds Dr Grindrod's comment: "Strange to state, passing strange, not one of these was a member of the Total Abstinence Society." Reports of the meeting were published widely, and Thomas Cook's *National Temperance Magazine* devoted several numbers to a full discussion of the arguments by both doctors, which was later published as a pamphlet. P.T.Winskill's comment on the end result was that it proved "the falsity and weakness of Mr Morris's position, and a triumphant victory for the principles maintained by Dr Grindrod."

Before the Spalding episode, Dr Grindrod had already met Thomas Cook in Leicester. This great pioneer of popular travel had been influenced by Dr Grindrod's old friend, the Baptist minister Francis Beardsall, and was a great supporter of the temperance movement. He was secretary of the South Midlands Temperance Association and his wife ran a temperance hotel, but his great contribution to the cause was the programme of railway excursions which did so much to popularise it in the area. His belief was that people could be encouraged to abandon their drinking when they saw that such excursions could be, as he described it, "a more attractive and wholesome form of recreation than the alehouse". The first big event took place at Loughborough on July 5,1841. The Leicester contingent paid a shilling for their eleven mile journey, and, accompanied by temperance officers and a brass band of several hundred, received an enthusiastic welcome in Loughborough. After refreshments of bread and ham provided by Thomas Cook, they returned to the station to meet delegates from Derby, Nottingham and Harborough. The whole party, "a colourful crowd, men and women, old reformed drunkards and young teetotallers from birth, sporting temperance medals, ribbons and rosettes, white wands and bright banners," then took part in a festive jamboree. The proceedings ended with some three thousand gathered in South Fields to hear speeches on temperance. Such gatherings were well established by the time of Dr Grindrod's visit to Leicester and help to explain why he got such a good reception here. His 1845 visit was especially remembered for his success with an audience of children and for its healing of discords that had recently arisen in the local Association. Internal dissension was unfortunately only too common in the temperance movement. Partly this was due to a genuine difference of opinion on the basic question of the merits of an anti-spirits movement versus teetotalism which was hard to reconcile. But there were many other factors, including the tendency of the movement to attract strong characters who felt that their personal prestige as leaders was a stake if they failed to win arguments for their points of view.

In the summer of 1845 there were some visits to the North, including Rotherham, Hull, Macclesfield and Doncaster. Then there was a further period in the Midlands which took in several Staffordshire towns. From here he moved to Cheshire, where he stopped at Congleton on his way to Cumberland, and here he visited Carlisle, Cockermouth and Whitehaven. The autumn period saw him in places as far apart as Sunderland and Leamington Spa.

The visit to Doncaster was reported very fully in the *Doncaster Gazette* (15 & 22 August) and it is worth looking at this account in some detail as it is typical of much of what was happening elsewhere. He was invited to Doncaster by a local committee of the New British and Foreign Temperance Society, who had been encouraged by a Mr William Morley of Hull to try to secure his services. It seems that owing to his many other engagements the committee had to write several times before meeting with success. Officially he had been booked to give four lectures, but in the event there was such a good response that he gave ten in all. The four scheduled lectures were held in the theatre on successive evenings (excluding Saturday and Sunday) to audiences ranging from about three hundred to fourteen hundred, with numbers increasing on each occasion. The evening sessions lasted three hours, and this included the lecture, followed by discussion. On the first evening he introduced the lecture by referring to the reasons which had led him to take up this work and describing some of the successes he had so far experienced. He also called attention to the various pictorial and other exhibits, and urged his listeners to note that these showed how alcohol transformed a healthy body into one that was diseased. In particular, he urged them to look at the pictures of the "grog blossoms" caused to the nose by excessive drinking, and pointed out the contrast between a healthy brain and a dark diseased brain affected with delirium tremens, or in popular terms "blue devils." At some length he challenged the view that strong drink was nutritious and quoted well-known authorities such as the German chemist Dr Liebig in support of his own case.

The second lecture concentrated on the effects of alcohol on diet and digestion and, with its lively anecdotes and powerful visual illustrations, it aroused great interest. Several other matters were included, such as the inadvisability of snuff taking and tobacco smoking, the importance of thorough mastication, and a recommendation of water as the only safe beverage. Washing daily from head to foot with cold water was also recommended. The meeting was interrupted by a former opponent of Dr Grindrod, who had since come round to agreeing with him as a result of his own personal experience, and the interruption was permitted by the organiser as it served to strengthen the lecturer's argument.

The third lecture concentrated on an appeal to the moderate drinkers who would have considered themselves far removed from the grog blossoms and blue devils fraternity. Physically speaking, he argued, the difference between them and the drunkards was only in degree, and many disabilities could be traced to moderate drinking. Parents in the slums, for example, gave their children small portions of gin and water to keep down hunger, but the main effect was to stunt their growth and make them weak and unhealthy. Drink was also an influence on cancer and cirrhosis of the liver, for it led to this organ being disabled from exercising its proper functions. In so far as strong liquor was a food, it was only fat that it fed and not a healthy state of body. As illustration of this point he alluded to a Mr Waterton, a thin spare man and teetotaller, who was noted for his agility and endurance as a traveller in the most unhealthy and dangerous places of the earth. Total abstinence was, in the doctor's view, the healthiest regime, and he appealed to his audience to pledge themselves to it and join the New British and Foreign Temperance Society.

The first three lectures had ended with questions being handed in, some of which were dealt with immediately, but as there had not always been time to take them all, Dr Grindrod began his fourth lecture by dealing with those that were outstanding. He then enlarged on the damage done to children's health by parents who were addicted to drink, and went on to discuss the effects of alcohol on the blood. Stomach, lungs and liver were then shown to be particularly at risk and he supported his case with many examples taken from his own practice as a doctor, besides quoting many of the leading medical men of the time. The circulation of the blood and the function of the respiratory organs were then demonstrated with a spirited commentary on his striking pictures. Again he appealed to his audience to come forward to join the Society and sign the pledge.

Very high on Dr Grindrod's priorities was the education of children. If their interest could be aroused, their enthusiasm was a key to the future and they had the advantage of not as yet having bad habits to break. Clearly he had a gift for communicating with the young and his success on previous occasions encouraged him to insist on meeting them in Doncaster. Two free lectures were given to children from nine to fifteen, and around a thousand attended at each session. The case for total abstinence was presented by dramatic anecdotes of the fearful consequences of indulgence in drink, backed up by lurid illustrations, and the children of the 1840s were just as appreciative of these as a juvenile audience might be to-day! More so, perhaps, for they had fewer opportunities to enjoy such a spectacle. He did not only appeal to the fear motive, however, as much of the lecture was a serious study of the functions of the human body and was primarily educational. A skilled teacher, he made sure that his message was grasped by the audience, and at the end of each session they were questioned on its contents. The newspaper report commented that "their ready and simultaneous answers gave convincing evidence that they were quite as capable of understanding the lecturer as many of more advanced years." Controlling such a crowd of youngsters cannot have been easy, and his management of them suggests he must have been an unusually charismatic personality. Some six hundred of these listeners were enrolled in a juvenile temperance society. To help them to be faithful to their promise, Dr Grindrod emphasised that there should be a follow-up in the form of meetings for instruction combined with various forms of entertainment.

Lectures to the ladies of the town were by now an accepted feature of every programme and Doncaster was no exception. As with the children, admittance was free, and the session which lasted two hours was well attended. While stating that the address was received with enthusiasm, the reporter was clearly much less interested in this event than in the public meetings which took place in the following week.

Because large crowds were anticipated, the Covered Corn Market was hired by the temperance committee, who took various measures to improve its facilities. Forms were provided as seating for the ladies, but after the first lecture the number of these had to be increased. Long pieces of cloth were hung round the sides of the building to reduce draughts, and the interior was lighted with gas expressly for the occasion. Such was the interest that had been aroused that crowds began arriving long before the appointed time of 7.30pm. The number was estimated at 1500 to 2000, and with people coming and going, silence was procured only with great difficulty. On the first occasion it was clear that the crowds were not immediately ready for a serious lecture, so a Mr James Backhouse of York was invited to speak. He had travelled, mainly on foot, some 6000 miles in South Africa and other countries, and the audience listened intently to his exciting tales of adventure, which ended with a commendation of cold water as the best drink for healthy living. Dr Grindrod then gave his lecture, with points similar to those he had made in previous sessions, and urged all present to aid the great moral movement already begun in Doncaster.

The atmosphere at this meeting gave cause for anxiety, and although there were police on duty outside the market, a number of those present withdrew, fearing an ugly scene. Mr Joseph Clark, who was one of those responsible for planning the event, told the crowd that there had been threats against Dr Grindrod and expressed the hope that antagonism should be directed against him and not at the lecturer. Dr Grindrod, to whom such opposition was no new experience, emphasised on his part that no threats "would deter him from doing that which he considered was for the reformation of society and the benefit of mankind," and stated that already since his visit began, upwards of eight hundred had signed the pledge.

At the next public session, the emphasis was on meeting the objections that had been raised, mainly by those engaged in the wine trade. Chief among the objectors was Mr William Price, a wine merchant who took exception to a statement he believed to have been made by Dr Grindrod, namely "that there were not half a dozen gallons of pure wine in Doncaster." Mr Price set in motion an acrimonious correspondence on the subject but was not prepared to accept an invitation to put forward his objections at a public meeting. Because of this the correspondence was read out by the chairman Mr Field at the evening meeting. Dr Grindrod's replies to Mr Field were on the whole firm but courteous. He stated that what he actually said was: "in my opinion there are not five gallons of pure unadulterated port wine – that is – the pure and simply fermented juice of the grape, in the whole kingdom". His definition of purity intended to convey the meaning that unlike much of the wine drunk in France, which was less intoxicating than the wine drunk in England, there were additions to the latter which rendered it "impure". Still less pure, in his sense of the term were the wines of Spain and Portugal, and particularly port and sherry. Mr Price had marshalled written evidence from many in the trade, who felt they were being challenged to defend the purity of their goods. He quoted statements from the Oporto merchants regarding the excellence of the Douro grapes and the care taken by the company to ensure that the farmers used only the minimum additives needed to preserve the freshness of the wine in transit. They did however admit that with so much wine involved there might occasionally be some adulteration, but if so this would be the exception rather than the rule.

Dr Grindrod in his reply produced a mass of evidence to the contrary. He quoted a Dr Charles Lee of New York who had remarked: "It is believed that the annual importation of what is called port wine into the United States, far exceeds the whole annual produce of the Alto Douro." Following up this allegation Dr Grindrod gave detailed statistics showing how imports to England over a period of eight years came from the Channel Islands; and whereas, for example, in 1826, 38 pipes were shipped to the Channel Islands from Oporto, 293 pipes were imported from the Channel Islands to London. Clearly additives must have been used somewhere en route to make up the shortfall. This conclusion, he added, was supported by a number of authorities on the history of intoxicating liquors, from whose books he then quoted extensively. He also drew attention to an admission in 1812 by the agents of the Oporto Wine Company that England did indeed have port containing additives: "The English merchants knew that the first-rate wine of the factory had become excellent; but they wished it to exceed the limits which nature had assigned to it, and that when drunk it should feel like liquid fire in the stomach, that it should burn like inflamed gunpowder, that it should have the tint of ink; that it should be like the sugar of Brazil in sweetness, and like the spices of India in aromatic flavour. They began by recommending, by way of secret, that it was proper to dash it with brandy in the fermentation to give it strength; and with elder berries, or the rind of the ripe grape to give it colour; and as the persons who held the prescription found the wine increase in price, and the English merchants still complaining of a want of strength, colour and maturity in the article supplied, the recipe was propagated until the wines became a mere confusion of mixtures." Not only was this true of port wine, he went on to say, but many other so-called wines drunk in England were adulterated with additives. In support of this statement, he quoted the *Quarterly Review*: "The manufactured trash which is selling in London under the name of Cape, Champagne, Burgundy, Barsac, Sauterne etc. are so many specious poisons, at the expense of the stomach and bowels of their customers." Not content with just quoting authorities, Dr Grindrod actually gave a recipe for the fictitious preparation of port wine, and exhibited some in a decanter prepared from spirits of wine, cider, sugar, alum, tartaric acid, and strong decoction of logwood, which had deceived several connoisseurs." Much of the argument between the two contenders was of a semantic nature turning on the definition of wine and the significance of the term additives. To Mr Price additives were for the most part beneficial and improved the quality of the wine: to Dr Grindrod they were adulteration that was poisonous in its effects. If his contention seems overstated to the modern reader, it is worth remembering that port and sherry were not at that time drunk in the small glasses with which we are familiar to-day but would have been drunk as freely as wine or even beer. Moreover the temperance reformers who took their stand on the anti-spirits position were happily drinking port and other fortified drinks on the assumption that these could not be classed as spirits. On this occasion Dr Grindrod had an advantage over Mr Price in that he was presenting his case in person at the meeting and while the audience might have appreciated that Mr Price had reasonable arguments, the sheer weight of contrary opinion quoted by the lecturer would have so bemused them that it would be likely to turn opinion in his favour.

Mr Price had not confined his attack to the actual arguments of Dr Grindrod. He also accused him of lecturing for personal gain. This charge Dr Grindrod refuted vigorously, drawing attention to the fact that of the ten lectures given in Doncaster he had received remuneration for only four. He had in fact "devoted the whole of his wealth to the extension of the principles of temperance, even to the sacrifice of private property." Another criticism by Mr Price concerned Dr Grindrod's drawings which he condemned as caricatures and accused him of "palming upon the gaping credulity of the audience." In his defence Dr Grindrod referred to a number of eminent physicians and surgeons, who had admired them, and in particular quoted the opinion of Douglas Fox, surgeon of the Derby Royal Infirmary, who had said he believed "there was not one of them by any means exaggerated. So far from it, they were extremely beautiful specimens of the diseases which they were intended to represent."

The final meeting ended with the audience predominantly favourable to Dr Grindrod and further recruits were added to the 40,000 who were already reported as having signed the pledge since his medical mission began.

In view of the hostility that his lectures aroused in some quarters, it was fortunate for Dr Grindrod and his wife that their hosts were owners of an estate at Marr, a little distance from the town. Arranging accommodation was often a problem, but here they received a warm welcome from Mr William Dent who was an enthusiastic supporter of teetotalism and became a close friend. Dr Grindrod refers to him and other members of the Society of Friends who had given them a hospitable welcome: "We had numerous hospitable invitations to private houses, and especially from members of the Society of Friends. How well I remember our visits to our dear friend William Dent, of Marr, near Doncaster, and his labour of love at all my meetings! Nor can I ever forget the kindness of the Tweedys of Truro-Vean, Cornwall, and a score of others, including the Tregelles, the Unthanks, the Bakers, the Alexanders, the Jarnons, the Foxes, the Wilsons, and others well known for their attachment to the cause of Temperance."

There were other times when a discreet withdrawal from adverse publicity was seen to be desirable. One such was at Newark in the previous year: "One of the most enjoyable visits we had for a week or more was at a cottage in Newark, whose owners were poor but pious, and whose flag-floored one room was our happy parlour. We had to take refuge there under peculiar circumstances, and the quiet and peaceful abode it afforded contributed much to lessen the more than ordinary severe trials I was exposed to in consequence of bitter and venomous opposition."[3]

Such opposition came mainly in places where vested interests seemed to be challenged and his Doncaster experience prompted him to consider the desirability of ensuring that from the first his lectures marshalled the evidence needed to counter attack the onslaughts of any potential adversary. A typical example of this was in his visit to Newhaven which followed within a week or two of the Doncaster events, and this was recorded at length in the *Whitehaven Herald* (August 30, 1845), which referred to him throughout as "the learned doctor." While giving positive instruction on health matters such as the process of digestion and the ill-effects of alcohol, even in moderation, a considerable portion of his lectures was directed at three groups who might wish to undermine his influence: those concerned with the drink trade; some of the clergy and religious persons who opposed total abstinence on the grounds that in their view it did not have the support of Scripture; and those members of the medical profession who gave a high place to alcohol in their materia medica.

Much of the material he had used to refute Mr Price in Doncaster was repeated here. After a comprehensive survey of the differences between many of the commonest varieties of drink, together with the etymology of their names and an analysis of their alcoholic content, he lined up a formidable amount of evidence to support his thesis that what passed for wine in this country had been through a process of adulteration which increased its toxicity. The range of this material was such that it would have taken a brave wine merchant to challenge "the learned doctor".

It was a great sorrow to Dr Grindrod that so many of the clergy failed to give wholehearted support to the principle of total abstinence. Nor was it easy for him to use the Bible itself in support of his arguments. True there were passages that could be quoted, but equally there were others that could be used against him. On this occasion he seems to have paid more attention to reminding his audience that teetotalism had arisen in a Christian land, among Christian people, and had the good results of reforming the drunkard, removing crime and paving the way to the conversion of souls.

Opposition from medical men was another topic on which he had much to say. Here he relied mainly on quoting the testimony of doctors who shared his own convictions on the use of alcohol. On a lighter note, he drew attention to the convenience of patients finding considerable reduction in their bills for medicine and medical attendance if they switched to a teetotal doctor. One such was "a highly respectable gentleman, a citizen of Chester, who as a moderate drinker was always subject to a variety of ailments, and whose bills for medicine and medical attendance, during a long period, were from £10 to £20 a year. He became a teetotaller, and for a period of eight or nine years, his accounts in that period did not exceed three-halfpence."

While giving a conscientious resumé of Dr Grindrod's lectures, the reporter for the *Whitehaven Herald* seems to have been as much interested in the man himself as in his message. He commented on his "soundness of argument, grace of diction, humour, and deep pathological knowledge." He noted particularly the way in which he dealt with questions: "with a tact and readiness which evinced much professional skill and an urbanity of manner that marked the Christian, the gentleman, the scholar."

What chiefly impressed him was the doctor's skill in presenting his subject in a way that could be understood by ordinary people: "The great obstacle to the elucidation of these subjects to mixed audiences has hitherto been found in the technical phraseology in which the science is shrouded; but to our surprise and admiration these lectures were rendered so plain that the meanest capacity could understand and appreciate them." Consequently, he noted, "The learned lecturer who was listened to throughout with almost breathless attention, concluded amid an enthusiastic demonstration of applause."

8

A Family Event

During the last week of 1845 and the first week of 1846 Dr Grindrod visited Worcester as part of his tour of the Midlands. Following the usual pattern, he came at the invitation of the local temperance societies, and the meetings took place in the Natural History Society's Room in Foregate Street. The four evening lectures were similar in content to those held elsewhere, with the emphasis on the aspect of medical education. *The Worcester Herald* (January 10, 1846), which reported them in some detail, particularly stressed the style in which they were delivered: "His delivery was calm, and his whole address argumentative, very different from the ordinary style adopted by lecturers on this subject; and if it be true, that he is the most successful advocate of the cause of temperance ever known in England, then we have another striking proof of the superior effectiveness of an educated and scientific address over one consisting of mere humour and ridicule; even though it be presented to the ears of those to whom such a style is thought to be most congenial." The attendance on every occasion was good, and it was noted that on one evening "several medical gentlemen" were present. On the final evening, the chairman, Mr H. Stone, proposed the vote of thanks, which was seconded by Dr H. Budd, one of the local doctors who had a practice in Foregate Street. While no reference was made to mass meetings, other than a tea meeting at Lowesmoor which was attended by about seventy, there was the usual afternoon session for young people.

In view of later developments in Dr Grindrod's career it seems likely that this would have been the occasion of his first visit to Malvern. He would have been able to take the four-horse mail coach from Worcester, although the serious flooding of the Severn at this particular time might have caused some anxiety. *The Worcester Journal* (January 3,1846) noted that the river at Tewkesbury was higher than was ever known in living memory, and described the scene from Worcester Bridge: "From Worcester Bridge the Severn looked like an inland sea, curiously dotted with lines of hedges, tops and upper parts of posts and rails, shewing themselves upon the face of the water." Once the travellers had covered the first mile or two the rest of the nine-mile journey would probably have been uneventful.

Malvern had recently become a centre for the practice of hydropathy, commonly known as the water cure, and this method of treatment, with its stress on the healing properties of water and particularly cold water, would naturally have had a special appeal to Dr Grindrod. Two of the pioneers, Dr James Wilson and Dr James Gully had been practising here since 1842, and at the time of Dr Grindrod's visit the former had just begun to set up what was probably the first purpose built hydropathic hospital in the country, which he named The Establishment. From the first the Malvern developments had attracted considerable attention in Worcester, much of it unfavourable, and a particularly acrimonious exchange in the press had taken place between Dr Charles Hastings of the Worcester Royal Infirmary and Dr Wilson. While Dr Hastings' opposition was partly influenced by his concern to preserve professional standards, there can be little doubt that financial considerations also supplied a motive, as the Worcester doctors were already finding that some of their patients were being lured away by the growing popularity of the Malvern water cure.

When Dr Wilson was a student at Trinity College Dublin he had come under the influence of Professor Macartney whose teaching on the healing power of water had made a deep impression. In later years he often recalled his professor's words: "If men knew how to use water so as to elicit the remedial results which it is capable of producing, it would be worth all other remedies put together." Dr Wilson's experience as a general practitioner, and even more as a patient himself, had reinforced this impression. During a period of serious ill-health he sought help from several leading specialists in England and on the Continent, but to no avail. Eventually he made his way to Silesia where Vincent Priessnitz, an Austrian peasant healer with no formal qualifications, was achieving spectacular results with the use of a variety of cold water treatments. For eight months he put himself under the Spartan discipline of Priessnitz, and also took the opportunity of learning from him the principles on which he worked while he observed at first hand the healer's daily routine. So convinced was he of the value of Priessnitz's methods that he determined to bring the water cure to England and establish it on the grand scale. On his return to London he succeeded in communicating some of his enthusiasm to his old friend, Dr James Gully; the two men visited Malvern and agreed that it was the ideal setting for their project. The village itself stood five hundred feet above sea level, and above the village stretched a range of hills from whose springs flowed an abundance of pure water. An added attraction was the gentle contours of the hills, which would enable even invalids to enjoy the opportunity of healthy exercise in the fresh air.

Dr Grindrod, who was four years younger than Dr Wilson, approached the practice of medicine with an open mind and would have been interested to learn about the water cure from someone with Dr Wilson's dedication and experience. It is probable that he visited him at this time, for in subsequent years when he came to live in Malvern the two men were good friends. Many of Dr Wilson's patients suffered from the poisonous effects of over indulgence in alcohol, that played havoc with their livers and rendered them helpless with gout and even more crippling maladies. Military men in both services, and particularly those who were stationed in tropical climates, figured largely among his patients, and the doctor was convinced that it was drink rather than the climate that ruined their health. Although not himself a supporter of total abstinence, he insisted on it as essential to his water cure treatment, and several months of water drinking under his strict regime encouraged many of his patients to abandon their high living in favour of a more abstemious way of life on their return home. Dr Grindrod would have been impressed with this confirmation of his own views, and he would also have heard reports of such benefits from his friend Joseph Livesey who had already experienced the water cure treatment. (Livesey's enthusiasm for it was responsible for the cartoon showing him carrying his hydropathic bath along the streets of Preston!)

Already the idea of setting up a practice in a place where this approach to medicine was acceptable must have had a strong appeal to Dr Grindrod. He was however at the time still too involved in his temperance work to embark on such a big change in his career, and for a while it was no more than a future dream.

In the summer of the same year Dr Grindrod took part in an event which was advertised as "A World's Temperance Convention" and described by P.T.Winskill as "one of the most important events in the history of the temperance movement." The National Temperance Society, based in London and operating on moderate principles, was host to this gathering; its aim was to draw together delegates from temperance societies throughout Great Britain and overseas, particularly in the United States. In view of the heterogeneous nature of the temperance movement it needed vision and courage to embark on such an undertaking. While the societies were united in their opposition to drunkenness they had little else to bring them together. Many were founded on a religious basis, but denominational differences were a divisive factor. This was especially so, since the Anglican societies tended to espouse moderation, while the non-conformist groups more often favoured total abstinence. This teetotal versus anti-spirits divide not only caused dissension between the various societies, but also threatened the unity of societies that accepted both types of membership. Another cause of friction was the attitude taken to the use of compulsion. In the United States there was strong support for controlling drunkenness by recourse to the law, while many of the reformers in England were uneasy about involving themselves in politics. In any event there was a tendency to resent any kind of foreign influence.

Despite the problems, three hundred delegates attended the four day convention in August 1846, which was held in the Literary Institute, Aldergate Street. One of the first speakers was Dr Grindrod and it is likely that he owed his invitation to his friend John Cassell who was one of those responsible for the planning. Dr Grindrod outlined the objects and methods of his temperance medical mission. He then described in some detail the reception given him in the places he had visited and spoke of his plans for the future. His contribution would have stimulated discussion as many delegates would have been unaware of this type of approach to temperance work. The interest shown by delegates from America led to an invitation to extend his mission to the United States, but unfortunately, owing to a period of poor health, he was unable to fulfil this engagement.

On the final day of the convention there was a gathering in Covent Garden Theatre, described in *The Temperance News* as "the monster meeting," in which leading temperance pioneers were the speakers. Amongst them was Mr Richard Allen, coadjutor of the famous Father Matthew, still revered to-day for his impact on the temperance scene in Ireland. Mr J.S.Buckingham, the MP responsible for the influential Buckingham Report, also addressed the meeting, and there was wide representation from America, mainly doctors and clergy, who contributed from their long experience of this type of work. Even at this early date temperance work in the United States was well ahead of that in England.

Soon after the convention Dr Grindrod continued his lecture tour, visiting some of the towns in the South East including Chatteris, Chelmsford, Colchester and Tunbridge Wells. Medical challenges were prominent on these occasions and the debate in Colchester particularly attracted attention.

Opposition to Dr Grindrod's stance on total abstinence came from Dr R.Chambers, physician to the Essex and Colchester Hospital. Dr Chambers submitted an article to the *Provincial Medical and Surgical Journal* (September 1846) "On Dilation of the Heart Consequent on Teetotalism," and the substance of this was widely circulated in the press. As in Spalding, Dr Grindrod took up the challenge. He investigated thoroughly the nature and history of the two cases recorded by Dr Chambers and his own diagnosis maintained that there was no heart disease at all. Twenty years later he again visited Colchester and tracked down one of these patients. He was found to be in sound vigorous health and still a confirmed water drinker, much to the delight of Dr Grindrod who was now in a position to confirm his earlier diagnosis. To have arrived at this conclusion on his earlier visit Dr Grindrod must have had access to the patients themselves and this is an example of what happened in many places. Patients who were dissatisfied with their treatment from doctors who prescribed alcohol found that he was willing to give them a consultation free of charge, and if appropriate provide an alternative prescription. It is hardly surprising that he made a number of enemies in the medical profession.

Some months after the original Colchester visit Dr Grindrod returned to the Essex area, and at Dunmow took part in a medical discussion that received wide publicity. On the first evening of his visit, April 20, 1847, Mr W. Cock MRCS and Mr John Coventry MRCS challenged Dr Grindrod's arguments on the effects of alcohol on the human body and particularly on the stomach. They presented their case very convincingly, and on the next evening Dr Grindrod produced a mass of evidence to support his original thesis. In the words of P.T.Winskill: "At the conclusion of the second evening's discussion a resolution was carried without a dissentient voice, expressing the opinion of the meeting that 'Dr Grindrod has demonstrated, by the light of science, and by a mass of evidence, medical and otherwise, of the most incontrovertible character, the truths of the propositions on which at the commencement of the discussion he based the principles of total abstinence.'"

A reporter from the *Medical Times* was engaged to report the discussion, and although his account did not appear in the publication he represented it was later published in a booklet of over seventy pages. Two months later Mr Coventry sent a letter to his adversary enclosing a portion of the stomach of one of his patients. After commenting on its condition he made the generous affirmation that "the evidence fully justifies your own views." This Dunmow discussion was notable for the high standard of debate. Much of it was extremely technical, with each side supporting its case with reference to a number of leading medical authorities. How much of it was understood by the audience is questionable, but no doubt they enjoyed the spectacle of warring doctors, however gentlemanly the conduct of debate may have been.

Soon after the first Colchester visit there occurred an important family event. After nine years of marriage Dr and Mrs Grindrod were still childless and as Mary Grindrod was now thirty-seven the prospect of starting a family must have seemed hopeless. Perhaps it was her pregnancy in the early months of 1846 that was responsible for their move to Niton in the Isle of Wight, which was one of the most popular spas in the country. Here their only son, Charles Frederick, was born on December 29; some months later, on August 29, 1847, he was baptised in St Catherine's Parish, Ventnor, where they were now staying. The considerable gap between birth and baptism seems unusual but it does suggest that they had quite a long stay on the island.

This part of the island enjoyed an equable climate, particularly in the Undercliff district between Ventnor and Niton which was protected from northerly and north-westerly winds by the Downs. The Gulf Stream helped to make the winters warm and with long hours of sunshine it was not uncommon for roses to be picked in January and primroses in December. Besides its mild climate Niton was famous for its Sandrock Spring which made the place one of the most desirable spas in the country.

Writing in 1841, A.B. Granville described the site of the spring: "The situation of the spring is extremely beautiful, commanding a view of the whole range of the Undercliff to the east, and of that part of the south-western coast of England we have so recently visited, to the west; while in front the wide expanse of the British Channel offers a never-ceasing source of attraction, in the numerous vessels and steamers that are tracking their silent way to and from distant climes." More important still was the mineral content of this chalybeate spring whose healing powers were recommended by local medical practitioners and others as appropriate "in a variety of cases of disease, especially such as are accompanied by debility, prostration of the nervous energy after long miasmatic fevers, and in many disorders of the female constitution."

Although only a small village, Niton offered accommodation at the Royal Sandrock Hotel and also in various lodging houses. It was not uncommon then for middle class families to take a suite of rooms for months at a time, where they could be accommodated with their own domestic staff, and it is probable that the Grindrods would have done this and perhaps hired their servants locally. With a population of about 5000, Ventnor had several hotels, but for a long stay the family would probably have rented rooms. A typical charge for this type of accommodation was two guineas per week for a sitting room and three bedrooms, with the use of kitchen and other facilities; in the height of the season the cost would rise to three guineas. One lady who stayed there with her daughter in 1841 commented that "the place is entirely occupied by invalids suffering from chest complaints, and every lodging was taken in the course of February." She adds, however, that better buildings were being erected, including three hotels, so by the time the Grindrods arrived it may not have been too difficult to find accommodation.

In the years following the birth of their son most of their temperance engagements were in the south of the country, and they worked their way west to places that included Exeter, Dorchester and Truro. Mrs Grindrod presumably left her young son in the care of nursemaids for long periods at a time, for it is clear that she still accompanied her husband on many of his travels. He refers, for example, to "a soaking journey on the coach in our transit from Exeter to Dorchester," which reminded him of another earlier adventure "over the Humber to Hull, when our limbs were so stiff with cold that a warm salt bath only restored sensation."

It was not unusual in this later stage of the tour for return visits to be made, and some of these took him back to the North again. Blackburn, which he visited in November 1849, marked his return with the gift of a full-size model of the human body. The presentation was made at a crowded public meeting by Joseph Brotherton, MP for Salford, who had long been a loyal friend and co-worker in the temperance movement. A written testimonial recorded that of the twenty lectures which Dr Grindrod had given, fifteen had been at his own expense. The gift was stated to be in acknowledgment of this and as a mark of "the respect and esteem in which the inhabitants of Blackburn held his services."

In March 1850 he was at Burnley. Here he was presented with two magnificent volumes of Dr Quain's *Anatomical Plates*, with a warm inscription on the flyleaf in which he was designated "The Medical Apostle of Temperance." Both gifts would have greatly pleased him, not least because this gesture at the end of his travels encouraged him to feel that despite a degree of opposition his work had been greatly appreciated. Writing some thirty years later, P.T.Winskill commented on the tour:

"Space will not permit us to give more details of these lectures and discussions, which, as previously stated, resulted in the accession of nearly 200,000 converts to teetotalism, and which certainly laid the foundation, in union with the prize essay *Bacchus* and other efforts, of the change in medical opinion, which is characteristic of the present aspect of the temperance cause. These discussions, which at this period (1840 – 1850) gained for Dr Grindrod the title of 'the medical apostle of temperance', took place more than thirty years before various of our distinguished medical advocates of the present day gave in their adhesion to the cause, and was carried on under difficulties and opposition which at this period of success can scarcely be realised."[2]

9

A New Beginning: Townshend House

In 1850, with the establishment of a medical practice in Malvern, Dr Grindrod entered upon a completely new phase of his career. It is true that he had already been in general practice in Runcorn and Manchester, but here there was a big difference. In earlier years patients had come to him or he had visited them in their homes. Now, although he still saw patients in this kind of way, the core of his practice was in his own home, where patients resided for long periods at a time, often months. Here they received constant attention and were encouraged to share in the whole life of the house as if it were their own family home. Moreover the type of medical treatment was different. While orthodox methods were not entirely abandoned, the emphasis was on the water cure, a form of treatment of which he had as yet no first hand experience.

A house suited to his purposes came on the market in that year. It was situated near the centre of Malvern and was less than five minutes

Townshend House 1850s

walk from Dr Wilson's fine establishment. The district, known as Southfields, formed part of the Nether Grange estate, whose owners, James Mason and family, had been selling large tracts of land from the 1840s onwards. These sales were accompanied by a very restrictive covenant. Only private residences were permitted and there was a specific prohibition of converting any building "into an Inn or Public House or Hotel for the sale of Beer or Cider or Spirits or into Tea Gardens or Livery Stables or other public places of amusement or resort or into an asylum either public or private for keeping insane or deranged persons." The siting of residences was also controlled, ensuring that no residence should be erected directly opposite or in parallel line with any other building. There was however nothing in the covenant that would have deterred a prospective buyer such as Dr Grindrod, and in fact most of its requirements would have had his positive support.

Townshend House[1] had already been built with these conditions in mind. Compared with Dr Wilson's Establishment, which had accommodation for over sixty patients, this house was of modest size. A house agent would no doubt have advertised it as "a gentleman's residence," but with the large families typical of Victorian times, it would have been able to house a dozen or more residents, plus domestic staff who would have shared the attic rooms. Its great merits were that it was set in extensive grounds extending to over two acres, and it had fine views towards the Malvern Hills, and in the north-easterly direction towards Worcester and the Severn valley. Situated at the junction of Radnor Road and Southfields Road (to-day College Road and Priory Road), it enjoyed a quiet position as there had been almost no development in this area and the covenant regulations ensured a minimum of development in the future. At a time when his finances were low Dr Grindrod would have appreciated that it was adequate for his immediate purposes, while if his practice prospered there would be scope for development. A lady who visited it in 1852 wrote to the *National Temperance Chronicle*: "The house of Dr Grindrod is plain but elegant, with a large garden well laid out, and abounding in the beautiful flowers for which Malvern is remarkable. The fine range of hills, at the base of which it is situated, offers constant attraction to the numerous visitors, whether on foot, horse or mule back. The situation is beautiful and healthy; there is an extensive view from the house over the fertile plains of Worcestershire and Gloucestershire, bounded by distant ranges of hills. On the west side of the Malvern range the country is more broken and diversified by gentlemen's seats, but not the less attractive." A similar description is given by the Rev Paxton Hood who visited it in 1858: "Compared with the vast establishments of the doctors in this place, Dr Grindrod's is but small, but the house is in most beautiful order, furnished in admirable taste, and from all that I can see, a most desirable place for a patient, who seeks, while prosecuting his health, tranquillity and calm. The grounds round the house are spacious, and well laid out, furnished with summer-house, bowling green, and means for athletic games, for those who choose to avail themselves of them. In this autumn weather it is very pleasant to sit beneath the shade of the veranda, if you are sociably inclined; or on the lawn beneath one of the huge trees, if you are disposed for solitude; and feel the gentle influence of nature and of the lulling winds falling upon you and soothing your spirit." The veranda mentioned by Mr Hood sheltered the lower rooms and made a pleasant break in what otherwise would have been a somewhat austere stone exterior. One of its greatest merits was an abundance of fresh spring water from the hills.

The Rev Paxton Hood was a Nonconformist minister, son of an able seaman who served in the Temeraire under Nelson. His book, *The Metropolis of the Water Cure or Records of a Water Patient at Malvern*, gives a valuable insight into life at Townshend House in these early years before the various extensions took place. While staying in the house he wrote a series of letters to a friend Sir George Sinclair of Thurso Castle, Caithness, and these were later collected and published as a book.

Arriving at Townshend House he was welcomed by Mrs Grindrod who immediately made him feel at home with a cup of tea (perhaps from the Leamington silver teapot) and a chat about mutual friends. It is interesting to see that her role as a hostess continued as in earlier days, although now she had the responsibility of looking after a three year old child. The lady who stayed at the house in 1852 also mentions her share in the running of the house: "The domestic arrangements of the house were excellent. Mrs Grindrod is a serious kind-hearted person who cares for and sympathizes with everyone." Visitors do not appear to mention Charles but since, according to the 1851 census, a nurse (nanny) Mary Thurston from Evesham and a nursemaid Elizabeth Orton were among the residents it seems likely that he spent most of his time in the nursery.

On the morning after his arrival Paxton Hood met the doctor himself, who was already in the dining-room when he came down to breakfast at 8.30 a.m. The first thing that caught his attention was a portrait over the fire-place which his hostess informed him was Vincent Priessnitz. He was already familiar with the fact that the water cure largely owed its origin to the work of this Silesian healer, but he had not before seen his portrait and it impressed him greatly. In his own words: "The calm, simple shrewdness, and quiet intelligence of the man's face is very fascinating to me, and reading the account of his discoveries, they seem indicative of the sure intuitions of genius."

Breakfast, and indeed all the meals, were a pleasant surprise: "I was prepared to expect in coming here rather a short allowance in the provision way. I thought our diet would be much plainer than it is. I find that the doctor maintains a perfectly generous table." While not specifying exactly what he ate at this and the evening meal of tea at seven, he does mention that there was oatmeal porridge, as no doubt this would please his Scots correspondent for whom it would be a "must". Unlike some other establishments, including that of Dr Wilson, patients were not expected to substitute water for tea. Some chose cocoa, but most, including himself, had tea, although he was less than happy that "the doctor has cut down my allowance to two cups, and those not over strong." At the 2pm dinner they sat down to "a well-spread table of good substantial meat in addition to game or poultry," and this was followed by various puddings, mainly tapioca, sago, bread and rice. Slow eating, allowing for thorough mastication, was encouraged, for in the doctor's view "no case of indigestion could be radically cured, except the sufferer acquired the habit of slow eating."

Breakfast and the evening meal were followed by family prayers. There was no chapel or special room set aside for this, so probably it took place in the dining-room. Townshend House was not unique among water cure establishments in making this a regular practice (it was customary, for example, at Ben Rhydding in Yorkshire), but it seems that the practice came in for some criticism in the town. Naturally, as a minister Paxton Hood defended the custom. He admired the doctor's sincerity: "There certainly is not the slightest approach to anything like cant about him," and he was emphatic that there was no compulsion to attend: "of course no one is compelled to be present when the bell is rung, yet I should think few instances have occurred of any one residing in the house who did not esteem it a privilege to attend."

After morning prayers Paxton Hood went for his first consultation with the doctor. The room, which was of modest size and called variously library, study, and consulting room, fascinated him, and while waiting he had time to look around and examine its contents. Two further pictures now caught his attention: an engraving of the Battle of Worcester, the original of which had been the work of one of the doctor's patients, and a portrait of John Dalton, the distinguished Manchester chemist, who had been the doctor's mentor and friend. Mr Hood was struck too by the wide range of the doctor's books, and noted that he kept his reading thoroughly up to date.

But what mainly absorbed Paxton Hood's attention was the vast collection of medical instruments. Many of these were what might have been expected of any competent doctor. Cases revealed dry cupping glasses, eye douches, chest inhalers, and a lancet, and he found himself wondering anxiously what a water doctor would want with the latter. A stethoscope and a spirometer also aroused his interest; but most of all he was curious about a beautiful mahogany apparatus, which served the dual purpose of enabling the doctor to weigh the patient and also check his height. A galvanic machine for transmitting electric currents and an instrument for administering oxygen also caught his attention, and he saw too the microscope which had been presented to the doctor in Blackburn. He was to learn in due course that patients were encouraged to use the latter and make discoveries for themselves, but for the moment he was overawed by the thousand and one things that showed the broad range of the doctor's mind.

This preliminary consultation made a deep impression. Paxton Hood liked the way in which the doctor enlisted his patients' co-operation by explaining to them the nature of their illness and the rationale of the treatment. He was to find soon that they were encouraged to extend their medical education by attending the weekly lectures given by the doctor on a whole range of medical topics, with special emphasis on the water cure. They were also given a booklet aimed at dispelling some misconceptions on the subject. On this occasion he was issued with a prescription for his first treatment which he was to find was a basic element of the water cure, namely the dripping sheet. Writing to his friend he complained, tongue in cheek, that the water cure lacked mystery. Not only were prescriptions written in plain English, without abbreviations, but they were even legible!

In between treatments which occurred at regular intervals throughout the day he had ample time to get to know his fellow patients. While the out-patients mostly lived in or near Malvern, the in-patients came from far and wide and represented a broad spectrum of middle to upper class life. Paxton Hood enlarges on this point and his description includes visitors as well as residents: "All sorts of people look in here, we rub off the rust and the dust of false notions and prejudices most admirably. Methodists, Quakers, Baptists, Independents, and Church people – baronets, colonels, captains, tradesmen, merchants, ladies of rank, and ladies who would like to be thought of rank – I have been in the company of all these, and seen them all together, since I have been here, sitting on the same sofa, chatting over the same book, entering with gusto into the same view or idea." The water cure at this time was so popular that there was virtually no rivalry among the doctors in attracting patients. Unlike

Dr Wilson, whose large establishment could afford to accept anyone who had the money to pay, Dr Grindrod was rather more selective, a wise policy for a smaller close-knit community. His many contacts throughout the whole country meant that he had a wide field from which to draw, and naturally he tended to attract many like-minded men and women. The clergy were particularly well represented, some of them local men. Hood noted this: "Seldom do you visit Townshend House, or range its garden, without meeting a number of clergymen, broken down by the excessive labours of their parish." Another well-represented group were men from India, particularly the military and those employed in the Civil Service and the East India Company, for the miracles of the water cure had become legendary abroad. Hood particularly noticed these: "Those sallow-looking gentlemen, that one, especially, whose step indicates the profession of a soldier; where do they come from, and under what form of disease do they suffer? They have been long residents in India, and are the victims of liver complaints. Whether it be climate, or good living, or both combined, I cannot tell; but one thing is evident, that what the doctor terms "the filtering machine" has not of late been performing its function. The skin tells a plain tale of an inactive liver, and the hue of the face marks the presence of bile, which the water cure alone can effectually remove. I have not unfrequently seen several "Indians" at once at the table of Townshend House, and the records of that establishment testify to the restorative effects of the treatment pursued." Medical men also presented themselves for treatment and this was particularly welcomed by the doctor. In his own words: "Since my residence in Malvern medical men have placed themselves under my care, and not a few have honoured me by their attendance on my weekly lectures."

Mr Hood was pleased to find that women were included in the company, a policy that had been repudiated by Dr Grindrod's contemporary Dr Gully, who had gone to the length of building a separate establishment for them alongside his original institution. Clearly Hood had him in mind when he wrote: "Glance for a few moments at another portion of the inmates of Townshend House, or the out-patients who ramble in the grounds – the ladies. Frequently have I stopped to gaze on a group of lady patients and their attendant friends. The voice of a female, even although an invalid, ever sounds cheerful to the ears, and often have I, in my moments of physical depression been soothed by a kind word and encouraging smile from one of the gentler sex, who seems never too ill to overlook the influence of sympathising interest . . . Imagine a gathering of male dyspeptics, or nervous hypochondriacs, assembling together day by day at the social board."

Children were also included among the patients, as Hood observes: "Look at a little child there in a perambulator, carefully attended by its nurse, with helpless limbs, a martyr to scrofula . . . No air like that of Malvern for strumous affections; no diet more likely to answer the end than the mutton fed on its fine hills, and the bread manufactured from the grain of its valleys. I have little doubt that the infantile sufferer will leave Malvern a different creature than when it came." In addition to the young patients, children played a part in enlivening the atmosphere of the house. Hood clearly enjoyed their visits: "For the last five years, the annual gathering of the parochial schools and clergy has taken place in the garden, by permission of Dr Grindrod. It is a beautiful sight to see 500 children on the lawn, almost every one with a bouquet of flowers, gathered from the cottage gardens, the clergy and ladies devoting themselves with earnest zeal and self-denial to the comforts and enjoyments of the 'little ones'."

On the whole the patients lived amicably together through the long stay at Townshend House. Social barriers that would have separated people in ordinary life tended to be broken down in the healing atmosphere of the place, a feature that Hood found quite remarkable: "Often have I watched with interest the harmony of intercourse and total freedom from caste, I have seen manifested by the noble lord, the honourable baronet, the titled lady, and the less aristocratic citizen, and as often have I felt proud at such an exhibition of *English* feeling. The stiffness of English society is a charge often brought, and sometimes perhaps too justly – but let such pay a visit for a few weeks to a hydropathic establishment, and they will be surprised at the ease and courtesy and kindness of daily intercourse of the great mass of patients." This phenomenon was not unique to Townshend House. Richard Lane, who was a patient of Dr Wilson in 1845, was no less surprised to find the extent to which social barriers were broken down at his first healing centre, Graefenberg House.

Paxton Hood did not of course pretend that there were never any problems. Not everyone was equally congenial, but those who did not fit in were the exception. There were for example the inveterate punsters who were apt to waylay the others at inconvenient moments when they needed an audience for the display of their wit. Such however could usually be avoided or at least humoured. Or there was the character, nicknamed Mephistopheles, an army captain who delighted in greeting his companions' remarks with a sneer: "a short man, and evidently tall in his own eyes; very dark black hair, sunken eyes and spectacles; a very tight lip, and supercilious twist round his whole face . . . all spiritual truth, all philanthropic thought – there was the same sneer."

Most of the patients joined in the various social activities that were organised for their entertainment. One that proved popular was the guessing game, in which the players had to elicit by a series of questions particular historical characters of the nineteenth century. Hood records one of his own efforts as a typical example:

Was he an Englishman?

Yes.

A member of the House of Commons?

No, but a very common character.

Was he a senator?

He was in the service of the state.

What was his profession?

A pause. A gentleman replied "He was a sort of general executor."

Was he a bad man?

The lady could not reply, but could say this, " that wicked people after they passed through his hands were wicked no more."

Had he published any books? Was he a literary character?

No; but he had been for many years engaged on some very public works.

What did he do then?

Well, he was greatly interested in the elevation of the lower classes.

This finally gave Paxton Hood the clue. He was Calcraft the hangman.

Hood was aware that this apparently aimless type of occupation was in fact part of the cure as it encouraged relaxation: "It is purposeless, aimless; but one of the most indispensable requisites of the course of treatment here is, that you shall throw off all courses of study, all courses of systematic reading; as far as possible, all the cares and annoyances of business. Just let the moments flit round you like tame linnets or canaries. Let the waves of life tumble round you like sunlit waves on a summer lake."

While party games mainly took place in the evenings, patients were encouraged to use the time between their water treatments for outdoor exercise, particularly on the hills. Not only was this to further their physical well-being, but also to give them mental stimulation in the study of the flora, fauna and rocks in the neighbourhood. Dr Grindrod had extensive knowledge in this field of study, and he liked his flock to pursue these interests and perhaps bring home specimens for identification. Allowing the use of his microscope, he opened up a new world of experience to many of them. Hood records his own fascination in watching the circulation of the blood in the web of a frog, an experience which so often is a first introduction to the delights of a microscope.

Paxton Hood expressed some disappointment that the hills did not present the challenge of Helvellyn, Snowdon and the Scotch Bens, nor the grandeur of the Lake District and the Highlands of Scotland. Nevertheless there were parts, particularly on the summit of the Beacon where magnificent views of the vast panorama could be enjoyed. Rejecting the mules and donkeys which were there to aid the less active visitors, he was happy to do his exploration on foot.

Sometimes he would stop for a rest on his expeditions. In his own words: "I have now been up several times, and three times in one day. I have loved to find some piece of crag or overcoping stone, and setting myself down there, take a book from my pocket, and read, or let the river of fancy 'wind at its own sweet will,' in reverie or in dream. It is very beautiful to notice how, as you pass along, the ground is broken into valleys, clothed with a short mountain grass and furze, and here and there the stunted trees, and many other characteristic objects, lending to the wildness and fascination of the scene. Thick high ferns cover the whole of the ground on one of these broken valleys."

There were areas of the hills that were a hive of activity. St Ann's Well was one of these. He writes to Sir George Sinclair: " I have just come from St Ann's Well. I wish you had been up there with me at six o'clock this morning, winding the way from the village (for I cannot call Malvern a town, although larger than many towns), attended as I went, by a number of travellers, some on donkeys, while numbers of young ladies, in uglies, most heroically breasted the difficulties with the walking stick, like a Swiss Jaeger. I came to St Ann's Well, and to be sure, what a festive scene the old place presented. A band was playing, as it plays every morning. A number of persons were assembled around the well, sitting, standing, or walking, but each and all occupied from time to time in drinking the water which trickles out of a marble mouth, into a marble basin in a romantic little room. The whole of the surrounding hills were alive with people. Far away, up to the heights of the Worcestershire Beacon, to which I intend walking to-morrow, the entire of the slopes and acclivities were thronged with multitudes seeking health, where health is truly to be found – from cold water, mountain breezes and exercise. I sat down charmed, you may depend upon it, by the spectacle, and my mind hurried away to the legendary times, when these saints' wells and holy wells were thronged by superstitious crowds in search of health and cure."

From time to time excursions were arranged for all the patients, and these were taken on mules, donkeys, horses, and rides in carriages for those who preferred less strenuous means of transport. Picnics were especially popular with Hood. These were organised with a drag, described by him as "a gentlemanly coach," and extra carriages if required. Eastnor Castle, residence of Earl Somers, and Croome D'Abitot, seat of the Earl of Coventry, were much appreciated, but best of all in Hood's view was Knightsford Bridge on the Teme which offered a variety of interests. He recalled one particular picnic which was undertaken in honour of a guest, Dr Grindrod's artist friend George Cruikshank and his wife. Described as the life and soul of the party, George enlivened them with recitations and story-telling, while most of the party joined him in song. Dr Grindrod improved their minds with a talk on ancient animal bones he had found in a sandrift quarry as they made their way to the banks of the Teme near Ankerdine. An open air picnic was then enjoyed, with ample provision for the hungry party: "The cloths were laid on the sward, the baskets and their contents were rapidly opened and distributed, the kettles were quickly boiled at the neighbouring cottages, and tea, and bread and butter, and cakes, and sandwiches, and fowls were dispatched in very pristine fashion."

During his three months at Townshend House, Paxton Hood had observed the progress of many of his fellow patients. While the healing process was mostly slow it could be remarkably successful. He notes, for example, a gentleman full of energy and animation, and adds: "You should have seen him three months ago, with a frame in a state of alarming emaciation, and with a countenance expressive of intense suffering. He had for months and years been a victim of neuralgia, or tic, and was almost worn down to a skeleton. Day after day, and night after night, was he subject to pangs of pain almost indescribable – to a state of torture which rendered death itself an object of intense desire. See what the water-cure has done for him, and again admit the efficacy of this life-restoring mode of treating disease." Even advanced stages of consumption could be helped: "I have seen cases under Dr Grindrod's care, apparently hopeless, in which the disease has been arrested, and life prolonged for many years." With regard to his own treatment he seems to have been well satisfied, and perhaps the best advertisement for his progress is the impression it made on Sir George Sinclair, for the 1861 census records a lady with the same surname from Thurso Castle staying in Townshend House, accompanied by her servant.

10
The Expanding Practice

The next visitor to leave a detailed account of what life was like at Townshend House was John Burns, an Irish supporter of the temperance movement, who stayed there as a patient in the early 1860s. While serious in his advocacy of temperance, his approach to the water cure was light-hearted and waggish, much of it concerned with proposing a musical setting to each item of the treatment. His roguish commentary was published in 1863 and went into a second edition two years later.

The title of his book is a clue to the nature of the contents: *Health and Pleasure or Malvern Punch*. There follows a lengthy elaboration:

Compounded of Spirits and Water and flavoured with
Things Geographical, Biographical and Laughable
Historical, Allegorical and Metaphorical, Geological
Physiological and Logical
the whole purified, liquified and intensified
by J.B.ODDFISH, ESQ. MP, LLD.
(Malvern Patient, Doctor of Laughs and Liquids)
(J. Burns)

Possibly the title owes something to a satire in *Punch* (Vol 11 pp243-4) entitled *Life at the Cold Brandy-and-Water Cure*, which tells of Mr Punch attending Dr Squilson and taking the "brandy and water" at St Cognac's Well.

Despite its humorous character the book throws further light on developments at Townshend House. Much has remained the same. The daily routine is similar and the author, like the Rev P. Hood, is just as appreciative of the food: "The breakfast is none of the scanty, half-and-half sort of things hydropathic breakfasts are usually supposed to be, but a good old-fashioned English breakfast, minus salt meats, mustard, pepper etc. The nonsense about brown bread, treacle and water breakfasts, has long since died out. The table here is full, free and hearty." One lady who, previous to coming, had only

Townshend House 1860s

taken green tea and fancy biscuits for breakfast was now able to tuck into a plate of cold beef and enjoy a cup of cocoa. Dinner, at which may be worn any dress "from a shooting frock to the uniform of a general," the company could sit down to "capital Malvern mutton, vegetables, fowls, puddings, pies and water." Second helpings were permitted: "That young lady passing her plate for a fresh supply of lamb was only this morning admiring the dear innocent little thing on the hills, and wondering how butchers could be cruel enough to kill them." Only "wine, beer and other artificial stimulants" were absent from the menu, as also were condiments on the grounds that they were bad for the digestion.

Apart from the fact that the house had by now been considerably enlarged and there were accordingly many more patients, those present still came from the same social milieu as those whom Paxton Hood had met. After enumerating a number of ladies and gentlemen without indicating their background, John Burns goes on to give more information: "The gentleman with spectacles is the popular preacher M. What a number of clergy frequent Townshend House. The one next to him is Sir T – an accomplished gentleman and no less accomplished scholar. The lady in conversation with him is Lady B – who charms every one by the urbanity of her manners and by her unwearying attentions and kindness to the more delicate invalids. Near to her is one of a different order of nobility, the wife of a cotton lord, but notable for good sense as well as good manners, with a mind stored with the fruits of a sound practical education. Lower down the table is a distinguished author, whose works have gained him a world-wide reputation; and by his side you see that quiet, unpretending, but intellectual looking man, one whose eloquence and thought have oftentimes riveted the attention of the House of Commons. From further afield have come an Irish General, a soldier, full of anecdote and courage, and of faith in the army of baths for routing any foe from the human citadel," also a gentleman from New York, whom he heard discussing the American war question. Burns was no less impressed than was Hood with their readiness to ignore social distinctions: "Thus you see them of all ages, conditions and complaints, chatting, eating, and drinking as members of one united family. All social distinctions are sunk in the desire to promote each other's happiness."

Shortly before John Burns's visit Dr Grindrod had been able to carry through the plans for development that he had in mind when he first bought the house. Clearly his practice must have prospered because no expense was spared in making it an ideal place for invalids. A new wing was added similar in size to the original building, thus providing increased bedroom accommodation, and the somewhat cramped and multi-purpose public rooms of earlier days gave way to rooms well suited to their particular use. The dining room, in particular, was planned on the grand scale. An article in *The Malvern Advertiser* (October 11, 1879) when the house had recently been re-decorated, describes it in glowing terms: "Next comes the dining room (50ft by 35ft), a room of splendid proportions, and on which the skill of the decorator has supplemented the comfortable arrangement of the furnisher. This is one of the finest private rooms we have ever seen, and certainly for a room devoted mainly to prandial purposes, it excels anything of the kind known to us. Besides the indispensable appendages of a dining room, capable of easily accommodating 150 guests, provision is made for every want which ease and enjoyment could desire or prompt, such as writing desks, couches, tête-à-tête and other lounges, easy chairs, etc, giving to the whole a quiet home-like air, which one hardly expects to find."

With the addition of the new wing the exterior appearance of the house benefited. While remaining of overall simple design it now boasted an impressive tower topped by a flagpole. Its construction may well have owed something to Dr Grindrod's memories of Osborne House, the Queen's mansion in the Isle of Wight. Climbing the tower to enjoy the fine view became a new entertainment for the more agile guests. Its erection seems appropriate for a man of Dr Grindrod's flamboyant personality, with his natural genius for showmanship.

The innovation that chiefly impressed John Burns was the splendid oval Winter Promenade, which he described as "a crystal palace in miniature, and by far the finest and handsomest room in Malvern." It was intended primarily as a place of exercise in winter

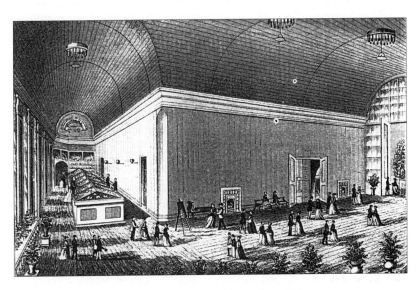

Interior of Promenade, Townshend House

or when the weather was too severe for outdoor activities. This building, a testimony to Dr Grindrod's imaginative approach to the practice of holistic medicine, is given pride of place in *The Malvern Advertiser* account: "At the end of the Museum is the Winter Promenade, a fine room, designed to meet a want generally felt in connection with Hydropathic establishments – where patients may take moderate exercise in immediate connection with such establishments so as to obviate the unpleasantness and even risk of exposure to a sudden change of temperature. No risk of this kind is run here; the patient passes direct from his own room to the Promenade, the temperature of which is regulated according to requirement. Here, too, are full-sized Billiard Tables, Bagatelle Boards, and other forms of recreative attractions, to help while away – what it is in too many instances felt to be – the dreary monotony of indoor life. Nothing can well be pleasanter than the comfortable and enjoyable life which the Promenade supplies to delicate persons, and especially in the winter, when the rigour of our English climate is softened to the temperature of Madeira or south Italy. Ferns and other plants adorn the Promenade and help to give it a cheerful aspect; and whether in the long days of summer, or the dark dreary nights of winter, health and pleasure go hand in hand in the Promenade." Adjacent to the Promenade was the Museum where the doctor's fine collection of medical, geological and natural history specimens could be housed in a setting that did justice to their unique character.

John Burns noted the good use made of so many of these innovations. Much of the light entertainment that was part of the programme in earlier years continued to flourish. The party games did not have to be limited to the drawing room. Now there was ample opportunity to expand into the Promenade, and patients who did not want to join in the family entertainment could make their way to the Billiard Tables and Bagatelle Boards, or indulge in battledore and shuttlecock. A musical man himself, John Burns particularly enjoyed the performances of the pianists and singers, not least when they entertained him with his favourite Irish melodies. In the evening it was still the custom for most of the patients to gather in the drawing room after tea and evening prayers, and the entertainment was not unlike what many mid-Victorian families would have organised at home. Amongst activities Burns lists the reading of a novelette by a lady who presented it "with wonderful humour;" a round game of "historical questions;" charades and chess in small groups; ladies who "ply their needles and conversation rapidly;" sacred music and parodies of well known songs, giving them a water cure slant. One of the latter was the Earl of Mornington's "Here in Cool Grot" which was followed by "Here in Cool Sitz" by a patient who styled himself the Earl of Evenington. The account ends: "Reader, good night. May all your days passed in the busy bustling world, amidst the healthy and wealthy, be as happy as those spent by invalids inside the walls of Townshend House, Great Malvern."

Amongst its many uses the Promenade became the venue for Dr Grindrod's medical lectures. These took place originally in a small room which Paxton Hood described as "an exceedingly neat, but not large lecture room, which subserves various purposes." This was often full to overflowing and admission had to be refused for lack of space. Now this was no longer a problem, and probably the continuance of his medical lectures was one of Dr Grindrod's biggest contributions to the Malvern scene. Instead of his countrywide odyssey, with lectures on a few days only in each place, he was able to deliver his teaching at a single centre to audiences drawn from all over the country and overseas. When originally planning to settle in Malvern he had this in mind, and it was his belief that the type of person visiting Malvern would be of sufficient intellectual calibre and influence to ensure the furtherance of his message.

A notice appeared regularly in the local newspapers advertising the subject for each Thursday afternoon, and as he was a stickler for punctuality it always included the words: 3.30 precisely. His biggest audiences were usually in the season from April to October, but in a good year the lectures were continued almost until Christmas. Weather permitting, they were sometimes held out of doors under the shelter of a spreading oak tree. They attracted widespread interest, as is shown by Paxton Hood's reference to those who attended when he was there:

"A noble lord of high conservative character, and a zealous Protestant; the notorious Irish malcontent and Roman Catholic MP; a lady eminent in the ranks of fictitious literature; a physician distinguished for his works on disease; a professor of anatomy in one of our large universities; a divine, whose eloquence ranks him among our highest of pulpit orators; a geologist, whose name is as widely known as the fossils are varied in the regions of Siluria; a gallant general, renowned for his martial campaigns; dowager ladies and spruce gentlemen; often a large sprinkling of the clergy." Hood then added the comment: "The Doctor evidently delights in these lectures. He often declares that he would rather resign a lucrative profession than abandon his privileges as a teacher, on the ground that it is more noble to prevent than to cure disease; and surely such lectures are of more than ordinary use in a place like Malvern, crowded with invalids, whose maladies are often brought on from a want of knowledge of correct laws, and not from wilful indulgence."

Although Dr Grindrod never lost sight of the issue of alcohol and its relation to physical health, the official advertisement called them Free Lectures on Physiology and the Water Cure. His topics covered the whole range of the workings of the human system, while the special emphasis was on the rationale and value of the water cure treatment. Amongst the many titles the following are listed: What is the Water Cure? The Baths and their Action; The Skin and the Water Cure; The Stomach and Digestion; The Stomach and Indigestion; Disorders of the Heart; The Brain and Brain Diseases; Disease of the Mucous Membranes; The Lungs and their Functions; The Heart, its Functions and Disorders; Warmth and Baths; The Brain and Nerve Disorders; The Liver and Bilious Disorders; The Water Cure and its Remedies; The Water Cure, its Modes of Action; Lung Disease and the Compressed Air Bath; Physiology and Digestion. The lectures, which lasted an hour and were followed by questions, were both scientific and popular. From his experience on his travels he had learnt the art of presenting scholarly material in an interesting way, supported by a wealth of illustration and hands-on use of apparatus. One of his patients, George Dew, who attended a lecture on

November 23, 1865, had a somewhat disconcerting experience. He wrote in his diary: "Went to Dr. G's and to his lecture in the afternoon, subject "Indigestion." When speaking of irritation of the mucous membrane and the furred cracked state of the tongue he said he had a patient there in the room but he would not make him a living specimen, whose tongue had cracks in it sufficient to lay a point of a penknife in and appeared as if it were divided into twenty parts. He said he was no draughtsman else he should have liked to take a sketch of it. He said also that this same tongue would be months, if not years before it regained it [sic] proper appearance. He referred to me I have no doubt: I saw him give a quick glance at me while saying it. He gave a rough sketch of it on the blackboard." That the doctor had a good sense of humour is indicated by another comment in George Dew's diary: "Went to Dr Grindrod in the morning and to his lecture on "Stomach Disorders" at 3.30 p.m.; he jokingly said he should not have but one or two more lectures this season because most of them would be at home at Xmas indulging in those very things which were the cause of his giving the lectures."

George Dew was one of Dr Grindrod's out-patients, who were able to take advantage of the enlargement of Townshend House. Not only could they now attend the medical lectures but if they so wished they could be accommodated for meals in the large dining-room, and also take part in much of the social life of the house. John Burns used to watch them arriving in the mornings for their consultations, and he noted with satisfaction that while some of the well-to-do arrived in their carriages, there was also a contingent of the "poor unpaying class of out-patients," who were treated "with as much skill and care as if they were able to pay in full."

Some of those who came from a distance preferred to find accommodation in the town, either because they liked their privacy or because the long stay required for the treatment made too great demands on the purse. Into this latter category came the two patients from Lower Heyford, George Dew and his Aunt Elizabeth. Aged eighteen at the time, George was the son of John Dew, a carpenter, builder, blacksmith and baker, and his father had provided him with a reasonable education in private schools. This had the effect of giving him an insatiable thirst for knowledge, and because of helping his father in the daytime he had developed the habit of studying far into the night. Poor health unfortunately undermined his efforts and he sought help from the family doctor. He wrote in his diary: "Mr Murchison tells me that medicines will relieve but not cure me. He doubts not that if I were to go to a cold water establishment at Malvern it should be cured."

Whether the doctor specifically mentioned Dr Grindrod, we do not know, but whatever the source of the recommendation it was most appropriate, for George Dew shared with the latter many common interests. He was a deeply serious young man, an Anglican but broad minded enough to attend the local Nonconformist chapels. He was, moreover, keenly interested in geology and other branches of scientific study. Above all he shared the doctor's detestation of alcoholism and its destructive effect on people's lives.

George and his aunt took rooms in Malvern in Leicester House, Imperial Place. This lodging house catered particularly for people taking the cure as it was fitted with the necessary facilities for having some of the baths at home. Owned by a Mr Samuel Langley, Leicester House was pleasantly situated near the station and from the sitting room window the two guests had a fine view: "We can see the grand Imperial Hotel & nearly the whole of Malvern, which is situated at the foot of those dark, high, brown, peculiar looking hills." Although there were about twelve residents in the house, they enjoyed a degree of privacy: "We do not see much of them as our staircase is entirely for our compartments." Malvern was an expensive town, a fact noted by many visitors, but this kind of accommodation would have worked out more cheaply than taking up residence in Townshend House. George's diary notes the cost: "Our lodgings and bath expenses are 16/- each per week so it depends on our living as to the rest." The food would have been cooked for them, but it seems that what was locally available did not altogether meet their needs as they sent home for the provisions that they particularly wished to have: "We want potatoes, apples & bacon & any other good things you have to spare.

Aunt E. wants a piece of bacon for breakfast: not too fat or lean . . . if you send a cake let it be a good one & not soda."

It was a pleasant walk of about one and a half miles to Townshend House and George visited the doctor about every four days to get instruction on the regime he was to follow. His stomach trouble seems to have been the main problem and this was accompanied by headaches, diarrhoea, depression and other unpleasant symptoms such as loss of appetite and extreme tiredness. His embarrassment at finding his tongue a source of interest at the lecture was at least less than that of some of Dr Wilson's patients who were liable to be confronted on their walks with a demand to put out their tongues for inspection!

George Dew followed conscientiously the instructions he was given regarding fresh air and exercise. Because of his poor health he sometimes found it necessary to use the donkeys, and he and his aunt would go for long rides together on the hills. One day he took a carriage ride, and like so many of Dr Grindrod's patients was greatly impressed with the beauty of the scene as they drove from the Wyche cutting down to the Wells Road: "If I attempt to describe the beauty of this road and the pleasure it gave us, I shall spoil the idea, for I am sure no writer would give a just representation of its beauties." As he regained strength he began to take longer walks and was able to manage the steep climb to the Worcestershire Beacon and even longer walks including one of seven miles to the Rhydd and back. Other guests from Leicester House accompanied him on some of his walks, including Mr Langley and his daughter.

During his long stay in Malvern which lasted over fifteen weeks, his health was variable, but at the end he expressed himself as reasonably satisfied with his progress: "The Water Cure has greatly relieved but not yet cured me. My tongue is coated still, though not so bad. If I take care I hope soon to be well."

John Burns seems to have been no less content with the results of his stay at Townshend House. His only criticism appears to have been that the musical entertainment which he so much appreciated should not have been confined to the hours of leisure only. It should have been a feature of the water treatment itself: "the time for music is during the bath – the place the bathroom." "Every bath attendant," he argues, "should be a musician and a vocalist as well. I do not mean to disparage the bath attendants at Townshend House, for they are, or were, the most obliging and attentive amongst the Order of the Bath, but Christy's Minstrels would, in some respects, make better bathmen under the new system".

11

The Water Cure and other Remedies

While most of the Water Cure doctors emphasised that their healing programme was a total experience, including diet, fresh air, exercise and mental relaxation as well as a variety of water treatments, clearly the latter had pride of place. To varying degrees the doctors also added other forms of treatment, some that would have been regarded as orthodox by the ordinary medical practitioner, others such as spirit healing, favoured by Dr Gully, and homeopathy practised by Dr Gully and Dr Stummes. Dr Stummes came as a partner to Dr Wilson in 1850, and in 1862 set up his own practice at Priessnitz House, a purpose-built establishment in the same road as Townshend House. Because of its preference for the use of minimal dosages, homeopathy had a natural appeal to some of the water doctors who were reacting against the toxicity of many popular drugs. Dr Grindrod, however, was not a convert to this method of treatment, and when accused in 1861 of practising it, he engaged in an acrimonious debate in the *British Medical Journal* defending his own position.[1]

In 1869 a Manchester friend George Wilson, a leading figure in the history of the Anti-Corn Law League, wrote to him asking for his help with one of his friends who was in poor health. Dr Grindrod replied with the following letter:[2]

Malvern. Novr 27th 1869

Dear Mr Wilson,

I received your letter & shall await any communication from your friend regretting as I do his unexpected indisposition.

Seeing that you are much interested in his recovery I pen a few lines out of my usual path.

I like to work <u>with</u> the ordinary medical attendants of a patient when I can do so – & most of my patients come from medical advice. I do not confine my practice to water remedies however valuable.

Patients may come down & benefit by a change of air – by the continuance of gentle remedies – & by mild & gradually adapted bathing. The warm water plan is essential to my cases & I introduced the practice into Malvern. I couldn't get on without it.

In cases such as your friend, I anticipate, that however valuable the local applications may be, the state of the general health will alone effect a cure. I have had them in every form and of the most violent character – but I have almost invariably found that in health remedies there was most to hope.

If your friend or his medical attendant would – at a proper time – write me some notes of the case – I could easily pronounce an opinion as to whether I could be of service or it would give me pleasure to run up to Windsor & see him & and to express my views after a personal examination.

Believe me,

Yours R

R B Grindrod.

The letter is of interest because it highlights some of the features of Dr Grindrod's practice. We can see from it that his aim was to offer a tailored treatment, insisting always on careful examination of his patients and consulting in each case where possible with the family doctor. Moreover it shows a holistic approach in which he set a high value on treating the person and not merely his ailment, and he did not confine himself to the use of water treatments only. His claim to have introduced his "warm water plan" into Malvern is open to question, but he certainly preferred gentler methods to the more Spartan regimes of some of the doctors. Since the water treatments now took central place in his practice and no two doctors administered them in exactly the same way, it is of interest to look into Dr Grindrod's own teaching on the subject and his particular approach, besides noting how his patients reacted to their novel experience.

The regular consultations which the patients enjoyed during their stay at Townshend House gave them the opportunity to co-operate intelligently in their own healing process, and like George Dew they might well have gained considerable enlightenment from the particular lectures they were able to attend. In addition, the doctor's own writings were available for study. Paxton Hood was issued with *Hydropathic Notes and Cases*, and some years later wider publicity on the subject was given in *Hints and Cautions to Water Patients*. After commenting on the latter that "this answered fully the purpose for which it was written," the *Birmingham Daily Gazette* (Oct 28 1865) went on to say: "Dr Grindrod is one of the ablest practitioners of the water treatment that we have . . . and for many years now he has successfully carried it out in one of the finest establishments which now adorn the beautiful locality." Even his guide to Malvern included detailed information on the water treatment, as indicated by its title, *Malvern. Its History, Legends, Topography, Climate, Springs, Natural History, with an Exposition of the Water Treatment, etc.*

A number of prejudices against the water cure were among Dr Grindrod's targets in his writings and lectures. The idea that it consisted simply of exposing patients indiscriminately to the shock of cold water applied in wrappings, douches and by various other means, was one that he particularly wanted to dispel. "The heroic water treatment is irrational and unscientific," he maintained, "the water remedies admit of endless modifications in relation to *temperature – force of application* and other conditions." Only if very carefully administered, with due regard to the reactive powers of the individual patient, could they be beneficial, and there were many cases where he did not apply cold water at all. Besides varying the temperature of the baths, it was necessary for the patient to observe certain precautions; for example, baths should not be taken when the patient was physically tired, nor should copious water be drunk in the same circumstances.

Two of the most basic forms of treatment were the dripping sheet (or wet sheet) and the pack. These had the advantage that they could be easily administered and even used at home. The dripping sheet was Paxton Hood's first introduction to the cure. Evidently he was adjudged strong enough to encounter it in its extreme form. At 5.30 a.m. he was woken from deep sleep by the bath attendant who enveloped his whole body in "a dripping cold wet sheet." After being rubbed vigorously in this, a dry sheet replaced it, and the result was: "I found my whole body in a most exuberant and healthy glow." He was then enjoined to take a two to three hours walk before breakfast. An alternative to the wet sheet was the pack. A wet sheet was placed on the bed, the patient wrapped up in it with only his head outside, and then a heap of blankets and other coverings wound around him. In John Burns's words: "There – you are bound hand and foot, like a sack of hops directed 'to be left till called for;' or a waxwork figure packed up for removal;- done into a mummy." In about an hour the unwrapping took place, and this was followed by the wet sheet procedure or a cold bath. With the final dry sheet rubbing came a wonderful "warm glow, a lightness, and buoyancy of body and mind."

Dr Grindrod had less enthusiasm than most of the doctors for the pack. He preferred to administer it only to smaller areas of the body rather than use a total pack. In his own words: "The entire wet sheet is a remedy used only in certain forms of disease, and in those cases where the power of reaction is vigorous and sound. In a large number of my successful cases the patient has never used the pack-*sheet* at all. The *partial* packings, however, in some form or other, I almost invariably recommend; as, for example, to the chest, the stomach and bowels, or to any portion of the body where the peculiar medical influence of that application may be required."

The sitz bath, which he valued highly, was the one which caused most entertainment to the patient, more particularly when he had the opportunity of observing his fellow sufferers undergoing the treatment. Sitting feet on ground, with the rest of the body wrapped in a blanket and only the lower part of the torso actually in the water, the patient presented a strange sight. "Hatching health" was what some patients called it, while John Burns preferred to describe it as "hatching eels."

The temperature of the sitz varied from ninety degrees down to sixty degrees, according to the reaction of the patient, and the water could be either still or flowing. Normally he could remain in it for anything from two to twenty minutes. According to Dr Grindrod it was efficacious for constipation, especially if accompanied by "brisk

Above: The Sitz

Right: The Douche

Below: The Pack

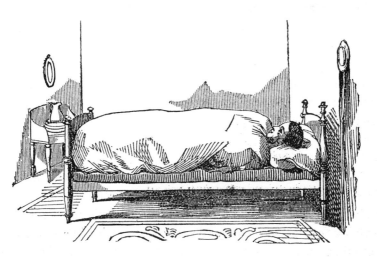

friction of the abdomen." Its sedative influence benefited the heart, and it was also helpful for headaches and various forms of mental disturbance.

Paxton Hood vouched for its soothing value once the initial dislike of it had passed: "I am not joking with you when I say that if you were to sit in it for twenty minutes a day it would cool your temper." He also felt that the indignity of it cut a man down to size. He tells the story of one man, an army captain, well-known as a writer, who as soon as he came into the house upset everyone by his domineering ways. "A pretentious jackdaw" and "cock of the walk" were his disparaging epithets. With some pleasure Hood noted the man's discomfiture when he surprised him in the bathroom "sitting and grunting on his sitz." To his moaning Hood replied: "Ah! my dear Sir, they are breaking you in." He adds: "My friend neither liked, I believe, my presence in the bath room nor my allusion." Hood himself found that reading a "tolerably fascinating book" made the experience more endurable, but he never got over its "remorseless ridiculousness." John Burns too found it comical, and amused himself by writing a parody of the song "I'm sitting on a stile, Mary."

Song for the Sitz
I'm sitting in this style, Mary,
The bathman by my side;
And if you saw me now, Mary,
You would not be my bride;
They call this hatching health, Mary,
I cannot tell you why;
There's water to my waist, Mary,
And water in each eye.

A treatment not considered by Dr Grindrod as appropriate for all patients was the douche, which could be used in various ways and with varying degrees of force and temperature. This "direct descendant of Niagara" as John Burns called it, had as its main objective to stimulate the system, but when applied with maximum force and lowest temperature it could have adverse effects if used indiscriminately. As Dr Grindrod observed: "I have known not a few patients lose all the advantages gained by a lengthened and judicious mode of treatment by the over-powerful stimulation of the douche... The larger sized form of douche is peculiarly stimulating in its effects, and requires to be carefully regulated. I have known it to operate on one unaccustomed to alcoholic stimulation, almost like a dose of brandy, rousing into momentary activity both body and mind, and if too long continued inducing a species of hysteria." He valued it however for its adaptability: "The douche admits of many modifications, both as regards force and strength of operation. It may be used of larger or smaller bore, and from a considerable height, so as to give great force in its application to any indolent surface where free stimulation is desirable. It may also be used from a more moderate distance, and with less vigour to surfaces requiring more delicate action, or in the form of a spray or shower bath, by the agency of a moveable tube with a rose affixed to its end. The spray or rose douche I often administer after a hot bath, and its effects are most refreshing and agreeable." Needless to say, John Burns had his own version of the perils of the douche, portrayed in both cartoon and song. The first verse is typical:

Cease to lure us 'bout the ocean,
Neptune's is an easy couch,
Listen while a fellow patient
Sings the dangers of the douche;
Stripped and shivering – quite defenceless-
Stunned by its terrific roar-
Now you're shouting – now you're senseless-
Now you're dashed upon the floor.

One bath that was generally popular was the lamp or sweating bath. According to Dr Grindrod the method was to burn a wick in a spirit lamp which was placed under a wooden chair. This was then surrounded by blankets draped over a cage in crinoline fashion which kept the patient comfortably warm and gently sweating. But he does also suggest a more Heath Robinson type of contraption which could be used at home. This was "a simple open tin, holding about 3 or 4 ounces of spirit, placed, in order to prevent accident if it should be upset, in a small bowl filled with water under a common, but large kitchen chair, with three or four blankets or rags thrown around." During the bath cold water should be drunk and the face and head sprayed with cold water, while after the bath some form of cold water bathing should be administered. John Burns had plenty to say on this treatment, which he summed up in the verse:

At present 'twould seem that they cure men by steam,

By means of new magical lights.

I'm broiled in hot air from that lamp 'neath the chair,

I know I'll be perfectly cured.

I'm going to expire! all the fat's in the fire!!

And the flames rising higher, fire! fire! higher! higher!

Going, – gone; and not even insured!

Foot baths, eye baths and a variety of other forms of water application were also among the treatments, and many of these were accompanied by massage, or, as it was more often called, shampooing. In Paxton Hood's words: "The couch in another part of the room is for the purpose of 'shampooing'. The doctor is very fond of the rubbing operations, and has usually several persons in his employ who rub, according to his directions, the spine, the back of the head, the limbs, the abdomen, or that portion of the frame which it is desirable to stimulate by hand friction."

While some treatments were administered in the patients' own rooms, most took place in the bathroom, one for the gentlemen and the other for the ladies. Here there was a large hot water tank, containing several hundred gallons of water, from which was supplied a variety of baths allowing for different depths of water. It was easy in such a room to provide the exact degree of temperature suitable for particular needs, and there was space enough for patients to move easily from one form of treatment to another. In the early days these rooms were alongside the main house, but with the developments in the 1860s they became part of the main establishment.

While all these treatments depended specifically on the application of water, another type of apparatus was introduced by Dr Grindrod in the 1860s. This was the electro-chemical bath, and he was probably the first doctor in Malvern to use it. According to John Burns, its object was "to extract, by means of electric currents, passed through the whole or part of the body, mercury and other mineral poisons from the bodies of those whose health has been nearly ruined by taking them." He records a comment of the doctor which he enjoyed: "the Doctor finds that quicksilver leaves the bodies of some patients more quickly than other silver leaves their pockets!"

A form of treatment which in Malvern was unique to Dr Grindrod was his compressed air bath. No other similar institution in England could at this time boast of such an innovation, with the possible exception of Dr William Macleod's Ben Rhydding Hydro

Compressed Air Chamber, exterior

in Yorkshire which introduced it at some period in its history. Dr Grindrod believed it to be an extremely important weapon in his armoury against disease. The enthusiasm which in earlier years he had shown in spreading the gospel of temperance was now given to another cause: popularising the new hyperbaric treatment among patients who might benefit from it and persuading the British medical world to take it seriously.

To this end he lectured and wrote tirelessly. It was the theme of many of his Malvern medical lectures, and he used his newspaper *The Malvern Advertiser* to keep the subject in the public eye. An early pamphlet, *The Compressed Air Bath* (1860) treats the matter in some detail, and a later book, *Malvern Past and Present* (1865), gives it even fuller attention, with the addition of excellent illustrations of his own apparatus. While these accounts were concerned mainly with the history of this type of treatment and a general introduction to his own use of it, a further book *Malvern; its Claims as a Health Resort* (1871) includes on its title page, "Also an Exposition of the Physiological and Therapeutic Influence of Compressed Air." Its concluding chapter devotes nearly forty pages to the subject, and this book too is well illustrated. By the time it was written he was able to use the fruits of his own experience to promote the cause, and the more personal approach adds to its interest.

The idea of using high atmospheric pressure as a therapeutic agent had been mooted first by an English physician Dr Henshaw in 1664 under the influence of Robert Boyle, but it was not until the 1820s to 1830s that hyperbaric treatment was fully developed by a group of French doctors. These included amongst others Emile Tabarié at Montpellier and Dr Milliet at Nice. Dr Grindrod's writings quoted a number of cases from these and other doctors showing how effective the treatment had proved to be for bronchitis, asthma, hooping (sic) cough, and phthisis in the early stages.

The compressed air chamber at Townshend House consisted of a complex of rooms. These were entered via the spacious promenade which provided shelter and warmth in bad weather and could be used for various forms of indoor recreation. It was particularly valuable for

Compressed Air Chamber, interior

gentle exercise before and after taking the air bath. A supply of books, papers and writing materials was available here for the use of patients, enabling them to pursue relaxing interests and so enter upon the treatment "in a calm state of mind." It was important that they should not indulge in too much physical effort, nor should they have recently taken a full meal.

The promenade gave access to two small rooms, one for the medical superintendent who had control of the machine which closed and opened the air bath, and regulated its pressure and temperature. A small glass window permitted him to view the patients under treatment. The other small room was the ante-air chamber which was available to patients who might feel the need to withdraw from the treatment during a particular session.

The main air chamber was a circular saloon, conical in shape, rising to a height of 14 to 15 feet and over 10 feet in diameter. The walls were of thick iron plates riveted together, and to make it appear less forbidding these were lined with wood, and there were several plate glass windows strong enough to withstand changes in air pressure. Pictures on the walls, chaises longues, chairs and a table gave the impression of a normal sitting room, and there was a bell with which the patients (who were fully clothed) could communicate with the medical attendant. Dr Grindrod was concerned that they should feel no tension, but rather come to regard the session as "a pleasant and agreeable conversational gathering as in an ordinary room." A session could cater for ten to twelve patients at a time, though occasionally they were fewer in number.

During the first half hour the pressure of air was increased to whatever degree was considered suitable for the patients' medical needs. This was effected by means of a steam-engine erected at some distance from the air chamber, which connected with a pumping apparatus. Underfloor pipes conveyed the air from "a healthy situation in the garden," and the procedure was so gentle that the patients were scarcely aware of what was happening. In Dr Grindrod's view, the ideal was "an increase of half an atmosphere or 7½ lbs of pressure on the square inch, in addition to the common weight of the air." This pressure was maintained for an hour and then gradually reduced over a half hour period to the normal pressure of 15 lbs to the square inch. Patients were encouraged to use the treatment not less than twenty to thirty times.

As with all his work, Dr Grindrod was meticulous in keeping records of the patients undergoing treatment and he approached the subject of cures in a strictly scientific way. Every statement about it in *Malvern; its Claims as a Health Resort* is backed up by detailed statistics, and he makes no extravagant claims. Analysing data from other practitioners, mainly French and German, as well as using his own observations, he sets out carefully what he believed to be its value.

Among the general effects were an improvement in the performance of the respiratory muscles, and increase in the capacity of the lungs, a greater absorption of oxygen, and the promotion of a more regular breathing rhythm. Consequently the treatment was particularly helpful for patients with asthma, chronic bronchitis, lung emphysema and other similar conditions. In severe cases of pulmonary consumption and other structural damage, only improvement rather than cure could be expected. He followed carefully a case of a 46 year old lady with advanced lung trouble and noted the relief afforded under treatment: "Each time when she entered the air bath the breathing was most distressing. Often she was bent double from asthmatic condition, and the features exhibited signs of the most painful disquietude. In a brief time very manifest relief was obtained, and in an hour I have often seen the invalid sitting upright in her chair and conversing with cheerfulness and ease."

Of prime importance in the healing process was the beneficial action of compressed air on the heart. It was Dr Grindrod's belief that many of the harmful drugs used to facilitate healthy action of the heart could be dispensed with. He quotes the opinion of an eminent physiologist Dr Burdon-Sanderson: "If there is a reasonable hope that by substituting a mechanical for a chemical agency we may be enabled to get the good without the evil, the experiment certainly ought to be made, not of course by sending patients to Reichenhall or Wiesbaden, but by having the apparatus in our London hospitals." Dr Grindrod's preference was to abandon diuretics, purgatives and other such medication, and replace them with this gentler form of treatment, and he drew attention to the types of ailment that would benefit from it. In particular he noted scrofula, anaemia, general debility, deafness arising from catarrhal infections of the Eustachian tube, and congestive irritation of the larynx, as well as the bronchial and lung complaints already cited.

In answer to the question of whether the effects of compressed air were permanent or temporary, he stated his conviction that unless organic disease was far advanced the effects could be expected to be permanent: "In a large number of cases, where there does not exist any formidable extent of organic disease, the effects must be permanent, – permanent because the direct influence of compressed air is tonic, and the secondary effect is to introduce into the blood an element which in imperfect lung-action it lacked – its natural and essential constituent."

While it was possible to claim that great benefits were derived from this form of treatment one basic disadvantage was the length of time that had to be devoted to it. George Dew's Aunt Elizabeth tried it for her deafness over the long period when he was undergoing the water cure. She must have had some faith in it as she returned for a second spell of treatment, but she does not appear to have been cured. However her deafness may not have been the type for which it was particularly recommended. Another first hand account of it comes from the pen of Mrs Dyne Jeune, wife of the Vice-Chancellor of Oxford University, who stayed for some weeks at Dr Wilson's Establishment in the autumn of 1860 while her daughter Margaret was taking the water cure. While there they decided to visit Townshend House as Dr Grindrod's innovation of the compressed air bath was causing such a stir in the town. Her diary records the visit: "One day we went to see a curious innovation at Dr Grimrod's (sic) and made by him – a compressed air bath for complaints of the lungs and chest. We tried it and found the effect most distressing and unpleasant – one felt as if one's head would burst, but I believe the boy attendant pumped in the air too suddenly. Anyhow it would be very disagreeable. The scene altogether was ludicrous." Such a reaction to what was Dr Grindrod's pride and joy would have been most distressing to him had he known of it, and one can only hope that her kind of experience was confined to the initial period of research into the workings of a new machine.

12

Townshend House: a Hive of Activity

While Townshend House was a place of healing, it was no less a centre for gatherings that represented the broad spectrum of Dr Grindrod's interests.

Temperance societies were always sure of a warm welcome to the house, and they included long established groups such as the Malvern Christian Temperance Society and the United Kingdom Alliance, which was one of those that favoured political action. A new arrival on the scene was the Good Templars. Founded in America in 1852, the Good Templars spread to England by the end of the 1860s. In 1870 the Grand Lodge of England was founded in Birmingham, and by 1873 it had become the largest in the world. In some of its principles, organisation and use of ceremonial, it owed something to the Freemasons, but it was far from being a secret society, and, unlike the Masons, it welcomed women. Its two main principles were: (1) total abstinence for the individual, based on moral persuasion, and (2) total prohibition of the traffic in intoxicating liquors for the nation. It aimed to achieve the latter by political means, supporting advocates of temperance regardless of their party affinities. Quoting from the Rev George Hinds, Right Worthy Grand Chaplain of the English Grand Lodge, P.T.Winskill defined its position: "This Order is a thoroughly uncompromising radical Christian temperance organisation . . . it makes a family circle where before there was disorder. It lays hold of the young at the most critical time of their lives and secures them to the ranks of total abstainers. It provides means of temperance, discipline and instruction, and in lodges, rightly conducted, true teetotallers may matriculate for the highest degrees and honours of virtue and sobriety. It is a valuable agency in watching the movements of the liquor-traffickers. It is intended to be the ally of all other temperance institutions, and leads the way to all reforms – personal, social, scientific and national. It enfranchises women, and is a splendid brotherhood – a compact family."[1] Like the Masons, it supported its own orphanages and was dedicated to giving mutual help to members, particularly in times of trouble or need.

A Malvern Hills Lodge was formed in the early 1870s, and on July 20, 1872, they organised a Demonstration of the Independent Order of Good Templars. Delegates from a number of lodges in the area gathered at Malvern Link Station, and set out, some 300 strong, to march to the Promenade Gardens accompanied by the Rhine Band. Dr Grindrod, who was not yet a member, was introduced to the delegates and invited to speak. According to the report in *The Malvern Advertiser* (20 July) this speech was preceded by "a glowing eulogium upon the eminent and memorable services of Dr Grindrod to the cause of the temperance reformation, for which he arduously and laboriously worked and pleaded before most of them were born." After several speeches the meeting dispersed, but re-grouped at 3pm on the Worcestershire Beacon. It seems from an article in the *Advertiser* that not everyone gave the movement wholehearted support. "Characteristic Americanisms" met with disapproval, in particular the "repulsive feature of female suffrage rampant in it," which the writer feared would have the effect of "transforming the quiet meek and homely maids and matrons of England into stump orators." Nevertheless Malvern soon had several lodges, and by 1881 the town could claim a total of 260 members. Not long after the demonstration both Dr Grindrod and his wife were initiated into the Malvern Hills Lodge and later he was promoted to a position of higher rank in the order. Undoubtedly the teetotalism of the Good Templars would have had an instant appeal, and his wife would have been given every encouragement to display her gifts of oratory if she so wished. Moreover the fact that the movement borrowed unashamedly from Freemasonry would not have been a deterrent, for only a few years earlier, on December 30, 1867, he had welcomed the Masons to Townshend House for the establishment and consecration of a new lodge, to be called Royd's Lodge. In proposing the vote of thanks, Sir E.A.H.Lechmere had been effusive in his gratitude, as recorded by *The Malvern Advertiser*: "Although accustomed to hospitality, they had never had a more cordial welcome than when they entered that house. Everything had been done for their personal comfort, and creature comforts had been plentifully provided. The room was most suitable for the occasion – a model lodge-room – and they must all feel a deep debt of gratitude to Dr Grindrod, and a hope that some day he might become a member of that Lodge, for his attainments, his kindness, and his readiness to help in every good work would make him a very good brother." It was not in fact very long before he was admitted as a member.

Gatherings in aid of religious causes were regularly included in the Townshend House programme of events. One such occasion was his support for the building of the new Wesleyan Chapel in Lansdowne Crescent in 1865, which replaced a temporary chapel on the site. The new chapel was in Early Decorated style, with a tower surmounted by four pinnacles, and built at a cost of some £3000. The land had been given by Mr Francis Lycett, who also laid the foundation stone. Both Dr and Mrs Grindrod were closely associated with the project and Mrs Grindrod organised a four day bazaar at Townshend House which raised £110. Bazaars seem to have been her forte, as only the previous year she had organised a two-day event to raise money for the improvement of the Countess of Huntingdon's Chapel. Similar support was given to another of their interests, the Vaudois Mission Asylum and Industrial School at La Tour in Piedmont. In 1853 two English ladies on holiday in the district had been alerted to the devastation caused by avalanches to the peasant families who eked out a precarious living on the slopes of the mountains. So distressed were they by the plight of the orphans that they founded a British Ladies Association to support this school which had been set up by the Waldensian Church.

Dr Grindrod's efforts on behalf of the Wesleyan Chapel did not imply that he had given up his allegiance to the Priory Church, in whose restoration by the architect Sir Gilbert Scott he had also been closely involved. It was made very clear that the Lansdowne Crescent Chapel presented no threat to the Established Church but was intended to provide a further means of spiritual instruction. The Priory, with its rented pews and central position, tended to attract the more well-to-do residents and also the hydropathic patients, while the Lansdowne Chapel was better placed for the increasing population in that part of the town. At the meetings connected with its foundation, emphasis was placed on its intention to be a centre for the preaching of "repentance towards God and faith in our Lord Jesus Christ," and this basic message of the gospel was one that specially appealed to Dr Grindrod at a time when the Established Church was in his view being threatened by the Tractarian movement. Not that the Priory Church was being undermined in this way, for Lady Emily Foley as its patron had ensured that only vicars of moderate churchmanship should be appointed to the living. However this was a period when there was considerable unrest in the Church, and Dr Grindrod, who was probably the author of the account of events published in *The Malvern Advertiser* noted that on Sunday mornings the Church of England liturgy would be used (i.e.matins), and that there would be no promulgation of "Popish or Tractarian views, nor the doctrines of Colenso, nor infidel teachings."

Missions at home and overseas that held their annual or other meetings at Townshend House are too numerous to examine in detail, but the following list is representative of the range of Dr Grindrod's interests: the London City Mission; the Irish Church Missions; the London Society for Promoting Christianity among the Jews; the Bible Society; the Church Missionary Society; the Colonial and Continental Missionary Society; the Church Pastoral Aid Society; the Bible Evangelical Missionary Society; the Chinese Missionary Society; the South American Missionary Society; and the Religious Tract Society. Most of these were evangelical in character and long established institutions, but societies that were formed to meet immediate needs were also represented. One of these was the Syrian Females Mission. This mission was set up in Hasbaya in 1866 where there had been several massacres of Christians by the Druses. These left many families bereft of husbands and fathers and led to extensive welfare work and the provision of schools for women, boys and girls.

An interest in education for people of every age accounted for many of the visitors to Townshend House. Paxton Hood had been delighted with the invasion of the children from the parochial schools who took possession of the grounds as an annual event. Other local schools enjoyed the same privilege. On at least one occasion the young pupils from Cheltenham Ladies College came for a visit. A more significant development was the provision of classes for boys and girls who were employed by the owners of the donkeys that were such a feature of Malvern at this time. From early morning to late evening the youngsters attended to the needs of the donkeys and vied with one another to get the custom of those visitors who were too frail or too lazy to walk up the hills. They were rewarded with only a pittance, but if they pleased their client an extra penny or two might come their way. Occasionally they could get time to themselves when the visitors had at last gone home, and Mrs Grindrod used this opportunity to put on classes for them on several evenings in the week. That this venture met with success is recorded in an article on Dr Grindrod in *The Templar*: "many of them, now grown up, attribute to that lady their gratitude for the only education they were enabled to obtain, and which has given them the means of elevation in life."[2]

Other educational and welfare institutions could be sure of a welcome at Townshend House, which lent itself to a variety of uses. The Educational Institutes of Worcestershire held their congress here, and on one occasion a concert was organised for the benefit of the Barnard's Green Institute. The organisers made a healthy profit which they attributed "largely to the kindness of Dr Grindrod who charged nothing." From time to time the house was used by the Malvern Working Men's and Literary Institute. Having had long association with working men's institutes from his early Manchester days, it was natural that he should support the Malvern Institute which he helped to found in 1861. He valued such groups, partly because of their contribution to adult education and partly because they presented an alternative to gatherings in public houses. In a vote of thanks to Lord Lyttelton, who chaired a meeting of the Worcestershire Union of

Workmen's Clubs and Institutes in 1879, he commented that he had "no faith in pothouse politics, or pothouse friendships, which often ended with broken heads." One particular group that had its headquarters at Townshend House was the Flymen and Cabdrivers Institute, which had an important role in a town like Malvern, which was flooded with visitors both for the water cure and as trippers when excursion trains were introduced in 1857. Its members appreciated having the use of a reading room, access to an extensive library and other opportunities of furthering their education.

There was also a lighter side to their connexion with Townshend House. Every year at Christmas-time the cab drivers, flymen, their wives and families and the donkey boys and girls were entertained to an evening party. In 1868 the numbers for this event were in the region of 200 plus babies. An onlooker described this gathering as "Somewhat noisy but by no means disorderly." After refreshments were served (the newspaper account mentions only tea, coffee and bread and butter), the Malvern Choral Society put on a musical entertainment, and there usually followed a magic lantern show. To whet their appetite for education various specimens of scientific apparatus were set out for them to explore, the most popular being a galvanic battery that produced electric shocks. Several speakers gave improving talks to encourage kindness to animals and arouse an interest in learning. A generous distribution of bread and butter at the end ensured that the visitors did not go home empty handed, but one can only imagine that they would have been happier if their host had not been a teetotaller.

With Dr Grindrod's particular background it is only to be expected that scientific interests would figure largely in the programme of engagements at Townshend House. John Burns notes that the museum was the centre of interest at a soirée held on November 16,1861, which was reported in one of the local papers. The report states that it was Dr Grindrod's intention to "permit, at convenient times, the free access of all geological students, and in addition to establish a School of Practical Natural History, with competent teachers or professors, who at suitable periods, will not only deliver lectures in the Museum,

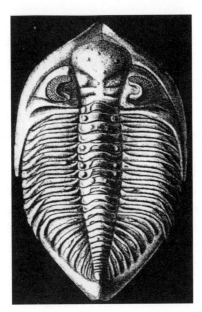

Trilobite: Phacops caudatus

but form classes for field labour, and visit in person the quarries and strata in the district." Although the plan did not materialise in any fully developed form, he did from time to time hold lectures here for young people, and he was himself invited in 1874 to give the inaugural address at the opening of the Natural Science Department in Malvern College. He also associated himself actively with its Natural History Society who hailed him as their "guide, philosopher and friend." On one occasion to their great delight he took them to a hither virtually unknown quarry where they were able to fill their pockets from a varied assortment of trilobites. A less happy incident was his offer to Mr Edwin Lees to take to London for identification an urn containing human remains that had been found in 1849 at the top of the Worcestershire Beacon. Assuring its owner of safe keeping, it was unfortunately years before he could find the precious object to return it to its owner.

13

The Museum

While Townshend House offered hospitality to people of wide interests, its most significant feature was undoubtedly the museum. Dr Grindrod's experience as a medical student under Thomas Fawdington would have made him aware of the value of a museum as a teaching aid, but it was only when he settled in Malvern that he was in a position to build up a collection of his own. While it included material that he could use in his medical lectures as well as a variety of objects illustrating the flora and fauna of Malvern, it became chiefly known for its geological contents. His fame as a collector was such that he earned a place in R.J.Cleevely's *World Paleontological Collections*.[1]

In building up his collection Dr Grindrod was clearly in the right place at the right time. While he was always on the look out to acquire material of interest, as for example the collection by Henry Brookes of Ledbury mentioned by Cleevely, he was living in Malvern at a time when the railway line from Hereford to Malvern was opened with its last section requiring the excavation of a tunnel through the hills. The work was completed by 1861 under the direction of Stephen Ballard, a local engineer, and according to John Burns, quoting from a local paper: "It is known to our readers that Dr Grindrod has for some years interested himself in the collection of fossils illustrating the Malvern district. During the progress of the railway works the last two or three years, unusual opportunities for the acquisition of geological treasures have been afforded, and the doctor has employed numerous men to disinter a large series of creatures who have been entombed for countless ages in the bowels of the earth; these specimens are now placed in the new museum, which is supplied with books, maps, diagrams, models, etc, in illustration."[2]

The museum attracted the attention of many of the leading geologists. Sir Roderick Murchison used it extensively in his book *Siluria* (1859) and J.W. Salter's monograph *British Trilobites* (1864) included some fine illustrations from his specimens. Dr Grindrod's patient George Dew spoke enthusiastically of the latter, who like him had rooms in Leicester House and was happy to discuss his work with a young man who was so keen to learn. Professor J.F.Blake of the University College of Nottingham was another leading palaeontologist who made extensive use of the museum for his monograph *British Fossil Cephalopoda Part 1* published in 1882. His preface to the latter, which specifically mentions his gratitude to Dr Grindrod, shows how such a collection was invaluable to anyone studying in detail the fossils to which he had access. After referring to his work in collecting information from other writers on the subject, he continues: "I then visited all the museums and private collections of which I had knowledge as likely to contain Palaeozoic Cephalopoda; and of every specimen which appeared to show any character, even though of a well-known species, I took by measurement and careful examination all particulars of size, shape, ornaments, and all other characters, assigning to each specimen a number. I specially sought out the specimens which had been used as types, which for the most part are still accessible, and carefully compared these specimens with all that had been subsequently written about the species, to see how far they coincided. I next copied on to separate sheets the actually observed characters of all the specimens which had been described as belonging, or seemed to belong, to the same species, whereby the wide range of variation which must be allowed under the latter title came out, and the best mode of grouping the forms was suggested; and where any doubt existed, I revisited the museum or collection, or in most instances was able to borrow the specimens for comparison . . . The work thus includes a description of every known *specimen* so far as it presents any available characters, or as I have discovered them. The total number of well-characterised specimens is about 2000, referred, as will be seen, to 143 species."

Before Dr Grindrod came to Malvern the district had already attracted the attention of Professor John Phillips, noted for his contributions to the *Memoirs of the Geological Survey of Great*

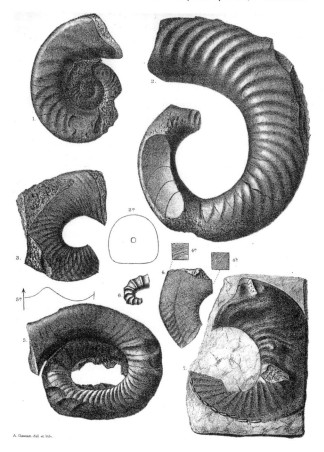

A. Gawan. del. et lith.

Fig.
1. NAUTILUS QUADRANS.—From the Lower Ludlow, Ledbury. In the collection of Dr. Grindrod.
2. TROCHOCERAS RAPAX.—From the Lower Ludlow, Ledbury. In the collection of Dr. Grindrod. *a*, outline of the radial section.
3. TROCHOCERAS STRIATUM.—From the Wenlock Shale, Garcoed, Usk. In the Museum of Practical Geology.
4. *Ibid.*—From the same locality and collection. *a*, magnified view of the surface near the convex side, showing ornaments. *b*, ditto near the concave side, showing epidermids.
5. TROCHOCERAS UNDOSUM.—From the Lower Llandovery, Llandovery. In the Museum of Practical Geology. *a*, outline of the sutures. Sowerby's type.
6. *Ibid.*—From the same locality. In the Museum of Practical Geology. A young example.
7. CYRTOCERAS (?) EQUISETUM.—From the Lower Ludlow, Ledbury. In the collection of Dr. Grindrod.

118

Britain. A letter from Dr Grindrod to Professor Phillips, preserved at the Oxford University Museum of Natural History, throws light on their friendship:

Townsend House, Malvern

Febry 5th 1857

My dear Sir,

Quietly and in my own name or that of a friend I am enquiring about a piece of ground or house with a view to naming it to you according to my promise – are you still in the mind at any future date to look at & consider an offer as to whether it would meet your views? It may be some time before one should offer but it is well to be on the look out?

The Berychia[3] I showed to you are about 4 in number

Berychia Kloedeni

Mundula

Bicornis

and

Siliqua

all of these are new to Malvern, but the Siliqua is new to Britain. It is likely that there are some other new varieties in my late gatherings but the above only have been examined. You did not see my very fine specimen of the Silurite Giganteus found in the immediate district, but only the cast of it.

I have a very accurate cast taken of it, but whether you will consider it worth your acceptance is a matter of doubt; are well-taken casts now discarded by geologists when the originals are scarce?

I am adding freely to my collection and in a few years shall I trust be able to exhibit a collection worthy of inspection. My intention is to devote it to local public purposes, in addition to lectures during the season. I need not repeat that when you like to make my house your home – and as often as you like – you will have a more than ordinary welcome. You can have your own room – avoid visitors – work up your books or lectures & be free from the formalities of ordinary guests.

Mrs Grindrod unites in kind regards to yourself and sister.
Believe me,
Yours faithfully,
R.B.Grindrod.

Reports of the various individuals and groups who made the museum a centre of interest enable us to build up a picture of its contents. Specimens of rocks were basic to the collection, and according to Paxton Hood, who had enjoyed the privilege of accompanying Dr Grindrod on geological forays, the hills were mainly composed of syenite. He went on to enlarge on this statement: "Syenite consists of quartz, feldspar and hornblende, which latter mineral is not present in genuine granite. Dr Grindrod has in his museum a very choice and unique specimen, exhibiting in one piece the four minerals, that is, those of which granite and syenite are composed. Any student in natural history may readily procure specimens by taking a brief walk on the north hill, the Beacon, or the district adjoining the Wyche. The slopes of the hills are covered with fragments of innumerable varieties of syenite, granite, greenstone, epidote, and silkenside, from the hardest rock, against which the hammer in vain strikes, to the most rotten and pliable, which is ready to become disintegrated into vegetable soil. Sometimes very fine crystals of hornblende are found, and of a peculiarly jet lustre, and now and then crystals of epidote reward the careful searcher."[4] A later letter written by Paxton Hood goes on to tell of the lectures given by Dr Grindrod on the subject: "The doctor at another time gave us a lecture on minerals and in particular the minerals of the Malvern Hills. He has a collection of Malvern minerals, pronounced by Professor Phillips to be the choicest ever made, and certainly the subject is of no small interest, and, dry as it may appear, can be made abundantly amusing to any inquiring mind."

Paxton Hood was familiar only with the original museum, but the extensions made to Townshend House in 1860 included a much more impressive structure and Dr Grindrod was now able to house satisfactorily his fast growing collection.

He was greatly pleased by a visit from the British Association for the Promotion of Science, who came in September 1865 when their main venue was in Birmingham. A large party whose special interest was geology spent the morning and early afternoon on the hills studying the metamorphic rocks at Wynd's Point and exploring the district of the railway cutting. They were joined by others for a 5pm meal at Malvern College, and afterwards some 100 members went on to the museum. Here their main interest was in the collection of Silurian and other fossils which had been set out in stratigraphical succession on various tables, one of which occupied the whole length of the room. The report in *The Malvern Advertiser* (16 September) noted particularly "fossils of Holly Bush Sandstone, Black Shale, May Hill Sandstone, Woolhope, Wenlock Limestone, Upper Ludlow, Downton Sandstone, and Old Red." Of special interest were the Trilobites, described as "exquisite specimens of these remarkable crustaceans;" the Crinoids "exceedingly choice and interesting;" and the Star Fishes, which included a new recently discovered specimen from Wenlock Limestone. The visitors who were less interested in geology were able to occupy themselves in a different room where various objects of Natural History were displayed and they had free access to a microscope. The visit ended with a vote of thanks by the Principal of Saltley Training College, seconded by Sir John Bowring, the prestigious Fellow of the Royal Society and at one time Plenipotentiary to China and Governor of Hong Kong.

From the time when Dr Grindrod first came to Malvern he became an active member of the Malvern Naturalists' Field Club, and this club together with the clubs in the district could always be sure of a welcome to Townshend House. A typical gathering was held on September 12,1866, when the Woolhope Naturalists' Field Club met in Malvern, together with the Cotteswold Club, the Malvern Club and the Worcestershire Club. The local club recorded it as "a grand gathering of Naturalists," and went on to say, "nothing could be better adapted to make it pass off well than the two or three hours of rain which fell in the morning, for it kept all the members together in the spacious Winter Promenade of Townshend House, where they first met, in full enjoyment of all that pleasant freemasonry of science, which is ever the charming characteristic of Field Clubs." Clearly the museum was on this occasion the focus of attention. "With such a gathering of the scientific men of the district it will readily be believed that the meeting was superior to the weather, and with Dr Grindrod's unequalled collection of Silurian fossils, a detention of three hours was positive enjoyment. No one could fail to be struck with the remarkable display of Trilobites, the perfection of the several specimens, or the graceful elegance of their forms in the varied positions in which nature has seized and preserved them for such countless ages. Dr Grindrod has spared no pains to get them together, and it may well be said that he has also been regardless of expense, for one little case, of the many there, the Doctor said had cost him fifty pounds."

Both lecturers at the 1866 Field Club gathering, the Rev H.Housman FGS and Dr Wright of Cheltenham, singled out for special mention the Silurian fossils, in particular, Lower Ludlow Star-fishes, Dudley Limestone Crinoids, and Trilobites. In Mr Housman's words: "Admirable as is the display of trilobites, that of the Lower Ludlow star-fishes, and Dudley limestone crinoids are equally splendid. Indeed we can imagine few treats more enviable to the geologist than that of an opportunity of studying at leisure this assemblage of Palaeogoric fossils, and surrounded by them, to acquire an intimacy with the strange and wonderful forms which dwelt upon the shores and beneath the waters of this globe whilst it was passing through one of the first of those measureless epochs by which, as by successive stages, it was being prepared for the habitation of man."

The Trilobites, however, seem to have attracted most attention. Mr Housman said of them: "It is however from the upper Silurian rocks that the finest and most abundant specimens in this Museum are collected. Of these, the series of Trilobites is especially remarkable. Glancing over them here collected together is a very real glimpse of the inhabitants of the Palaeogoric seas. Amongst others, we may particularly mention a group of the rare species

Sphoerexochus mirus, of which, until the forming of the Malvern Tunnel, only three specimens were known. Equally fine, too, is a group of the delicate *Encrinurus punctatus*, – so delicate that an individual with its projecting eyes, side spines, and back spine was till lately quite unheard of. Here, however, are more than a dozen in a state of absolute perfection, some coiled up as if taking a nap, others apparently walking towards an enemy with spines erect, breathing, as it were, both defence and defiance. Trilobites of all sizes are gathered here from the mud of the primordial oceans, from the minute *Cyphaspis*, with its long spines, to the gigantic *Homalonotus*, 6 or 7 inches in length. The most jealous care in selecting only the finest specimens has resulted in magnificent tablets of the choice *Cheirurus*, *Lichas*, and *Phacops longicaudatus*, and its variety *Grindrodianus* – named in honour of Dr Grindrod;[5] while groups of that excessively rare and precious Trilobite, the lately-discovered *Deiphon* and *Staurocephalus*, excite the wonder of the Palaeontologist."

As might be expected John Burns let his imagination roam freely over the Trilobites, ending his account with verses based on the song "The Jolly Young Waterman."

Oh, did you ne'er hear of a jolly young Trilobite
That lived in Siluria, once on a time,
And some years ago turned to stone in a terrible fright,
And forgot all about the deeds done in his prime.
But harden'd and horny his tail no more wags
For he now lies entombed in the Lingula flags.

Some doubt as to what was the cause of his fright,
Some say that the sea where he lived got too hot
Some say too cold, and some vanished quite;
But one thing is certain, whatever is not
That harden'd and stony his tail no more wags,
For he now lies entombed in the Lingula flags.

The jolly young fellow has had his day out,
And doubtless once relished like others a spree,

Made love to the Lingulas roaming about,
Was lively and affable, funny and free,
But harden'd and slaty his tail no more wags,
For he now lies entombed in the Lingula flags

While Dr Grindrod would have enjoyed John Burns's extravaganza, he was less concerned with the frolics of the Trilobites than with the more sober consideration of their witness to the omnipotence of their Creator. Like so many religious scientists of the time, challenged as they were by Darwinian theories of evolution *(On The Origin of Species* was published in 1859), he lost no opportunity to draw attention to his faith that science and religion were not incompatible. Dr Wright also voiced this view in his lecture at the Field Club meeting when he spoke specifically of the fossils: "If it was true that hundreds of thousands of ages had rolled away since these creatures lived, the same laws that governed their being, regulated their life, and assigned them their place in creation were presiding over the countless beings of the present time; and were it possible to realise, in a material form, the words of scripture, that the Author of our being was the same yesterday, to-day and for ever, he would point to the Crinoids, the Star-fishes, and Trilobites of the Silurian seas now before them, and say: "There are the evidences which declare the truth, and prove the reality of those all-comforting words."

14

The Malvern Advertiser

In Manchester, and in his travels throughout the country, Dr Grindrod was forcibly struck with the value of the press in furthering the temperance cause. It was natural therefore that when he settled in Malvern he would use it to promote the many causes dear to his heart. How better to do it than launch his own newspaper? So within five years of his arrival the town had its own local paper *The Malvern Advertiser*, with Dr Grindrod as its proprietor and editor. It was published by Mr William Barnes of 1 Edith Walk at an initial cost of twopence.

During the first few years from 1855 onwards, publication was limited to the summer months. It consisted then of four pages only. The first carried advertisements; the second dealt with home affairs, mainly reports on Parliament and the House of Lords; the third contained foreign and colonial news; and the fourth concentrated on Malvern. He was at this stage very dependent on advertising, for the cost of setting up his practice at Townshend House had been considerable and he had little spare capital. It is therefore interesting to note that despite his strong views on alcohol, he was prepared to accept advertisements from wine merchants. Some appear regularly; as for example, Walter Green & Co, Wine Merchants & Wholesale Bottlers of Malt Liquors, 4 Holyrood Terrace; also Messrs Archer & Son, Importers of Wine and Spirits, adjacent to the Foley Arms. At one point he refers to the fact that he had undertaken the paper at the urgent request of some of the principal tradesmen.

In June 1859 he appealed for the support of visitors and residents, both as subscribers and advertisers. He stated that the paper's publication was "to supply the requirements of the visitors and as a medium for Advertisement so that on first arrival in the town everyone may learn a little about the place and the different houses of business." The contents of the Malvern section would have been of practical use. It has lists of houses, including those that accepted lodgers and patients; and there are separate lists of physicians, surgeons and vets, also of churches and chapels. Details are given of the various means of transport, together with the fares. But his intention was also to help residents and visitors appreciate the beauties of Malvern and the rich variety of its flora, fauna and geological treasures. Extensive articles on these topics are included, which he eventually incorporated into his books on Malvern. In 1865 he published *Malvern Past and Present*, and some years later followed it up with *Malvern; its Claims as a Health Resort*. He also included at various times articles on the water cure and other medical subjects, with a view to helping patients co-operate intelligently in their treatment.

In 1860 he decided to extend the period of publication, and after stating in October that the new paper was particularly needed in the summer months he went on to say "We shall not discontinue *The Malvern Advertiser* with the dying year, but keep fully alive even through the dark months, that we may open a spring campaign with renewed vigour." It seems likely that this development was prompted by the arrival on the scene in the previous year of *The Malvern News*. The proprietors, Parry & Co, also owned *The Worcester Journal*, until in 1864 Joseph Hatton took it over and sent Josiah Morris, who was on its literary staff, to be manager of *The Malvern News* and later its editor. Some time in the 1860s Dr Gully took over as proprietor. He continued to employ Josiah as manager and editor, although his own contribution in the latter field was considerable.

By 1865 *The Malvern Advertiser* had been enlarged to eight pages. News from Ledbury and Upton was classified separately, and a regular feature with the headline Portfolio was introduced and used to present edifying proverbs and religious quotations. In popularity the paper was able to hold its own with its rival *The Malvern News* but it was very different in character. The latter had strong political interests and supported conservatism, whereas the *Advertiser* was independent and more concerned with social questions. In the words of its editor: "Social questions are those in which we avowedly take deep interest; we leave political differences in the main to our daily contemporaries." (Significantly there is no mention of its weekly contemporary!).

Relations between the two newspapers and their respective editors were far from amicable. References in the *Advertiser* to "our little contemporary" and "our feeble and quarrelsome neighbour" were hardly calculated to please the *News*. But these were provoked by a challenge from the *News* of the accuracy of the *Advertiser's* report on the cataloguing of the British Museum Library. Since the *Advertiser* prided itself on careful reporting and was able in this instance to refute the charge, it was hardly surprising that its language was unflattering.

A more serious attack came in May 1864 when an anonymous letter, with the heading "A Medical Curiosity" appeared in the *News*, objecting to the award of the Lambeth degree of MD. Its source was clearly Dr Gully. It was prompted by a question that had been put to the Home Secretary by Colonel French asking if it was true that "the Archbishop of Canterbury possesses the power to create Doctors of Medicine, without their having undergone previous medical education and examination." The letter pointed out that a Lambeth degree is always mentioned with a sneer in medical society," and since Dr Grindrod was the only physician in Malvern to possess such a degree the letter was clearly intended as a stab in the back for his colleague. In his reply, Dr Grindrod commented that the letter was "cruel, mean, dastardly, and ill-judged, and was one of many efforts to lower my medical status and impugn my professional reputation." Expressing "deep humiliation at being dragged into a professional controversy," he made it clear that the Lambeth degree was not for the purpose of creating him a medical practitioner, but as a special mark of esteem. Several columns in the *Advertiser* were devoted to the argument that whereas Dr Gully had the advantage of a medical degree from Edinburgh, his own qualifications, though different, were no less valid, and he explained in great detail the history and significance of the Lambeth award.

This contretemps was not the end of hostilities between the two doctors, for in 1867 Dr Gully was again on the offensive, using his own Edinburgh degree to belittle his rival's qualifications. After a long drawn out war of words which raged over several months, the public eventually got tired of the controversy. A letter in the *Advertiser*, signed Knowles King, who called himself "a subscriber", voiced the general view: "there has been enough of the Gully Grindrod controversy . . . no two medical gentlemen in England are more loved as men and respected for their professional skill by their friends and patients than are Dr Gully and Dr Grindrod." The new editor of the *Advertiser* endorsed this view in the following week and added his own opinion on medical men's connexion with the press: "Let doctors mind their physic and their patients; one doctor has retired from active connection with the press; it would be a blessing if others in Malvern would follow so wholesome an example."

While Dr Grindrod was still editor of the *Advertiser* the reporting of current events was regularly followed up with a moral homily rather than a discussion of the political issues. The ending of the American Civil War in 1865, for example, inspired a leading article expressing satisfaction that slavery would be abolished, but also a concern that America would not be tempted to embark on further conquests but would "add to the common welfare of mankind." This emphasis on promoting welfare recurs again in his comments on the successful launching of the Atlantic Cable in the same year. What, he asks, are to be its commercial and social results, and is it destined to be geared to the promotion of peace?

Another event of 1865 was the death of two statesmen, Lord Palmerston in October and King Leopold of the Belgians in December. Both had played a leading part in guiding the troubled affairs of Europe during these mid-Victorian years. In his leading article of December 16, Dr Grindrod, prompted by the recent death of King Leopold, paid tribute to their work, referring to Lord Palmerston as "the far sighted" and Leopold as "the European Umpire," but the main theme was a lengthy homily on the deaths of great men as a lesson for human pride.

Nowhere is Dr Grindrod's claim that social questions are a deep interest more evident than in his reports in 1865 on children's labour in the Potteries and among the brickmakers of South Staffordshire. The same crusading zeal that led him to expose conditions in the Manchester and other factories is now shown in the treatment of these subjects which he believed should be understood by the people of Malvern who were their not too distant neighbours. On the evidence of the inspector of factories, Mr Baker, he dwelt on the scandal that nearly 4000 children under thirteen were employed in bad conditions in the Potteries. The plight of the brickmakers of South Staffordshire was no better. Here nine to twelve year old girls were carrying weights amounting to over sixteen tons in a ten-hour day. Of these he wrote: "We must care for their bodies as well as their souls, and we must interfere, by legislative enactment, if need be, to protect labour from the tyranny of capital; and above all, we must redouble efforts to promote among the masses that 'Godliness with contentment is great gain.'"

The nailers of Northampton also attracted his attention. In particular he noted that the law limiting the work of children, inadequate though it was, did not even apply to the iron-working types of employment. While he expressed a preference for reform through moral persuasion he was sufficiently pragmatic to appreciate that legislation was often the only answer. The amount of column space given to such topics ensured that the message could not be ignored.

Reform of working conditions in Malvern also had a place in his social crusade. While there was a movement aimed at requiring shops to close at 7pm and he urged his readers to co-operate in this, he reminded them that even this was inadequate since it would mean twelve hours business was still permissible. He drew special attention to the fact that the late hours in winter would mean exposure to "the pernicious influence of gas," and so would be injurious to health. He appealed to the ladies of Malvern not to delay their hours of shopping and to avoid shopping after 2pm on Saturdays, thus encouraging the shop owners to accept earlier closing hours. The postmen too had a champion in the *Advertiser*. Here the cause was as much religious as social. In response to a movement in several towns to guarantee postmen a day of rest on Sunday, the editor informed his readers that he could supply a form to be filled in, stating "I will not trouble you, in future, to send my letters etc on Sunday." The cab and fly drivers also found in him a champion with his appeal to the Town Commissioners in 1865 to build them a shelter at the station or give them permission to move to the shady side of the road.

Exposure to physical danger, particularly in employment, was a cause that had priority. He drew attention, for example, to Queen Victoria's plea in connexion with a railway accident in 1865 that "the same security may be ensured for all as is so carefully provided for herself," and he endorsed the move in 1860 to provide harbours of refuge to reduce the danger to shipping. The transport of dangerous goods on the roads was another issue on which he had strong views, and when in June 1866 there was a Bill before Parliament on the Carriage of Dangerous Goods he was to the fore in organising a petition from the people of Malvern to the House of Lords pointing out that it did not go far enough. The Bill covered railways, ships, and public conveyances, but not public thoroughfares, and a recent accident in Malvern had brought home the horrors of inadequate provision in private employment. For weeks the newspaper gave details of the plight of the Wallis family. The father Robert Wallis, who was a haulier employed by the Worcester Chemical Works, had taken his wife and two children with him when he was transporting twelve glass carboys of oil of vitriol from Diglis in Worcester to Holy Well in Malvern. Just past the Foley Hotel a heavily laden carriage crossed his path, and then, trying to take avoiding action, the two horses took fright and overturned the dray, upsetting its contents and throwing the family on to the road. The whole family suffered appalling burns. The three year old boy died within three days, and the seven year old girl not long after.

Dr Grindrod and three other doctors gave first aid, removing the casualties to the Skittle Alley of the Unicorn Inn, and a few days later he supervised their removal to a room at 2 Saville Row, where accommodation had been found that would at least give them some privacy from the gawping crowds. Here they were cared for until their condition improved sufficiently for them to be taken to their home in Worcester. With the aid of a few helpers Dr Grindrod organised a fund to meet the expenses of their care and provide support until their claims for compensation could be met.

The accident happened at a time when plans were afoot to provide a cottage hospital for Malvern, and the inadequacy of the arrangements for the Wallis family highlighted the urgency of such provision. The *Advertiser* had done much to promote the venture, and now Dr Grindrod proposed that if any money over and above the family's needs should be contributed, this surplus should be transferred to the Cottage Hospital Fund.

The health of the town was high among the newspaper's priorities, and besides promoting the plans for the hospital, many other concerns were given prominence. Amongst them may be cited the need for a properly run Market Hall, the provision of a cemetery outside the residential area, better housing accommodation for the poorer inhabitants of the town, and the provision of public parks to replace the Link Common and Malvern Common. The latter, which came to nothing, was directed against the encroachment of commerce into areas that should be preserved for recreational use. In 1865, for example, attention was drawn to "the sides of the hills being recklessly defaced by quarries; gravel pits making sad havoc of our commons."

With its ever increasing population, sanitation was a perennial problem for Malvern. The *Advertiser* kept a watchful eye on the situation. An outbreak of cholera in Southampton in 1865 caused its editor to draw attention to the need for vigilance. Commenting that the disease was the "the natural offspring of filth, intemperance and other similar conditions," he made a number of practical suggestions, including a demand that pig styes and other offensive buildings should not be sited near main roads. An appeal to the housewife was also made. She was reminded of the importance of cooking meat properly: "We do not know that a roasted parasite is less wholesome than a roasted sirloin, but to introduce a living traitor into our stomach citadel is the height of folly and may turn out to be a most unpleasant bore."

The *Advertiser* had plenty to say on the activity or non-activity of the Town Commissioners with regard to sanitation. In spite of all the springs on the hills the water supply, particularly in the summer months, often gave cause for anxiety. One of Dr Grindrod's nearest neighbours, Dr Stummes, used its pages to voice his complaints. When Dr Grindrod first came to Townshend House, the road that became Radnor Road and later College Road was no more than a track, but by the 1860s it was a proper thoroughfare and housing was beginning to be developed. Having set up his water cure establishment, Priessnitz House, Dr Stummes was soon finding that he was faced with problems. In 1865 he wrote to the Town Commissioners complaining that the water which they supplied was full of sediment and unfit for culinary purposes, a very serious matter for a doctor trying to run a water cure property. Their reply was far from encouraging, for he was merely told that the house was at the end of the main and the discolouration came either as a result of recent rains or the action of water on pipes.

With increasing need for storage tanks and proper facilities for sewerage, matters came to a head in 1866. The Commissioners, who were unwilling to court unpopularity, were trying to excuse their inadequacies by maintaining that they were not sufficiently empowered to take action and needed a new Local Government Act to enable them to carry out the necessary developments. Dr Grindrod took a different view. In his opinion a new Act was neither desirable nor necessary. The existing Acts contained every provision needed, and it was the failure of the present Commissioners to use wisely the money already at their disposal that had precipitated the crisis. To postpone action would mean a delay of at least two years and the situation was too serious for that. What the Commissioners needed was to enlist the services of more experts, and even if this meant a rise in rates, it would be better than no action at all. A protest meeting of ratepayers was called to discuss the Commissioners' proposals, and columns of the *Advertiser* were devoted to undermining their arguments. The end result was their defeat, with the Commissioners resigning en masse. Perhaps it added a little to Dr Grindrod's satisfaction that Dr Gully was Chairman of the Commissioners. The latter used his own newspaper to belittle the meeting as "a miscellaneous crowd of ratepayers and non-ratepayers" and dismissed their vote as emanating from "a lickspittle populace and press", a charge which the *Advertiser* disputed vigorously.

If the editor of *The Malvern Advertiser* was reticent about entering into party politics this was certainly not true of his treatment of religious affairs. Here he had to defend himself against the charge that the subject had too prominent a place in his newspaper. On November 17, 1866, he wrote: "We have been blamed in some quarters for introducing religious and ecclesiastical matters into our columns. It is said that such topics are unsuited to a secular newspaper." In his defence he referred to the London daily papers and in particular quoted a recent example of a letter from Dr Pusey in *The Times* on the subject of the use of confession in the Anglican Church.

Sometimes it was local matters to which he drew attention. Churches and chapels in the town could always rely on good coverage of their day to day events, and this was specially so when new ventures were being planned such as the building of the Wesleyan chapel in Lansdowne Crescent. But inappropriate practices did not escape attention. An example of this was his attitude to pew rents in the Priory. Strongly opposed to them, he seized his opportunity when in 1864 a letter had appeared in the paper accusing the verger, Mr W.E. Gwynne, of receiving gratuities from visitors seeking good seats. Mr Gwynne denied that he had received any solicited gifts, but did not deny that he had accepted some that were unsolicited. Dr Grindrod then joined the debate giving his own views in no uncertain terms: "I am determined in every way in my power to abolish the disgraceful practice of paying or receiving money for a seat in God's house on God's day," The matter came up again in the following year. This time the subject of pew rents in the Priory was raised by the secretary of the Liverpool and Birkenhead Open Church Movement, who expressed the Movement's displeasure at the custom. After allowing some free discussion of the subject, Dr Grindrod then closed the debate with his own powerful and lengthy condemnation of the practice.

Much of his polemic was directed against the influence of the Oxford Movement in the Anglican Church. He was prepared to accept the place of Roman Catholicism in other countries, but set himself against its progress in England and particularly against what he saw as the infiltration of its tenets into the Established Church. This was mainly on the grounds that in his view it undermined the responsibility of the individual for his own beliefs and actions. Long columns of the newspaper were devoted to the question of the use of confession at the time when Dr Pusey had been defending it in the columns of *The Times*. Dr Grindrod was willing to concede that it should not be forbidden, but he argued that those who wished to use it and adopt other similar practices should not remain within the Anglican Church. In his own words: "Do not practice it within the bosom of the Protestant Church of England. Go where such things are allowed, but stay not where they are in spirit if not in letter forbidden."

Anything that undermined religious faith incurred his condemnation. The Colenso case in 1862 was given prominence in the *Advertiser*. After nine years as Bishop of Natal, Bishop Colenso published in 1862 the first part of a book *The Pentateuch and Book of Joshua Critically Examined*, which challenged current orthodox interpretation of the Old Testament. It raised doubts about the historical existence of Moses and treated Joshua as a mythical character. This radical approach, coming from a responsible bishop, created a great stir in Anglican circles, and he was excommunicated by his Metropolitan, the Bishop of Capetown. Bishop Colenso refused to resign from his see, and in 1865 his refusal was upheld by the Judicial Committee of the Privy Council. Another bishop was consecrated and for the period until Colenso's death there was schism. Dr Grindrod devoted many columns of his paper to explaining that the decision of the Privy Council was not in any way an endorsement of Bishop Colenso's heretical views, but purely a legal decision, since the Bishop of Capetown did not have the authority to act as he did. In supporting the Bishop of Capetown the Crown lawyers had blundered, with the result that the Queen in issuing Letters Patent had exceeded her powers.

But it was not only from within the church that the faith was being undermined. In the same year a paper read by Mr Winwood Reade to the Anthropological Society of London was severely critical of missionary efforts among native populations. A number of letters for and against the thesis that the Anthropological Society necessarily supported unscriptural views appeared in the *Advertiser*, and after allowing free discussion Dr Grindrod capped it with a very long leader on *Infidel Attacks on Christian Missions*. This was directed not so much against the Anthropological Society, which he was prepared to admit presented a variety of views, as against the particular theme of Winwood Reade. His argument was that far from damaging the African converts to Christianity, numerous examples could be quoted showing that missionary work had resulted in all kinds of educational, moral and religious benefits, and that medical missions in particular had brought untold benefits to people's lives. He referred to this article in a later number, expressing his conviction that the newspaper "had lately vindicated the result of Foreign Missionary efforts against the attacks of scientific infidelity."

On August 31,1867, a notice appeared in the *Advertiser* under the heading Change of Proprietors and Change of Editors. The reason for the change is then given: "Growing professional engagements have hastened the resignation of our Editor under whose guidance *The Malvern Advertiser* has attained a position of influence, rarely paralleled during a comparatively short career. The impossibility of constant residence in addition to failing health, has induced the Proprietor to avail himself of a favourable opportunity for transferring the business to a gentleman competent to do it full justice, and to devote his whole time to the service of the public." The new proprietor, Mr John Sloggett Jenkins, assured his readers that the policy of the paper would continue as before, and he reiterated this claim in exactly the same form in several subsequent issues. Dr Grindrod's assistant editor "M.A." was now promoted as editor.

The reference to Dr Grindrod's failing health is the first hint of the heart trouble that was to make life difficult for him in his later years. But there is no indication that at this time he expended any less energy on the rest of his commitments, and an immediate sequence to his resignation from the *Advertiser* is that he was able to give time to writing another book. *Malvern: its Claims as a Health Resort* appeared in 1871, and the enormous amount of research which underlies it would have been difficult for a busy newspaper editor to undertake.

The notice of his resignation as editor reminds the readers of some of his objectives for the newspaper, one of which was "promoting the interests of the town and district." It has been shown already how well he realised this aim, and the new book was undoubtedly planned to promote the interests of Malvern. It was of course to his own advantage to attract visitors to the water cure. Spas on the Continent were becoming more accessible to the middle classes as the developing network of railways was making travelling cheaper, and this same development was making the fashionable spas of England easier of access and therefore making them a counter-attraction to Malvern. But his treatment of the subject was not merely due to self-interest. It sprang from a genuine love of the town. He had put down his roots here, and there is an unmistakeable warmth in the way in which he treats the subject.

His claims for the merits of Malvern are presented in the Preface. While admitting that special circumstances may make it right for some people to seek health in other places, his conviction is that "England can claim to be the healthiest country in Europe . . . and I think that the present volume will show that Malvern is the healthiest climate in England." Whether he proves his case may be disputed, but if arguments backed up by an impressive use of statistical evidence can be trusted, his views must certainly be respected.

The book begins with a description of Malvern's geographical position, noting the variations in height over the whole eight-mile range of hills. The six localities with the name of Malvern (Malvern Link, North Malvern, Great Malvern, Malvern Wells, Little Malvern and West Malvern) are described in detail, and in some cases their heights are noted. For example, Great Malvern 500 feet, Malvern

Link 200 to 250 feet lower, North Malvern mainly 650 feet, and Malvern Wells 550 feet. A geological survey then shows that the composition of its earth is favourable to "quick and effectual infiltration, in this way preventing accumulation of stagnant water" and moreover it possesses a rocky stratum "which favours the retention of warmth from the rays of a genial sun."

In his examination of the vegetation he points out the many species that flourish in Malvern because of the favourable climatic conditions, and especially its freedom from frosts. He quotes conditions in the winter of 1859-60 when "numerous shrubs were destroyed in the low plains between Malvern and Worcester, while not a single specimen of the same plants suffered in Malvern itself." This observation is backed up by a quotation from Edwin Lees in his *Botany of Worcestershire*: "Though in the severe winter of 1859-60 numerous laurestines, bays, arbuti etc, were totally destroyed in Devonshire and Herefordshire, and also in the lower parts of Worcestershire, and rose-trees were killed by thousands, yet about Malvern scarcely any destruction of shrubs took place. This immunity from intense cold is attributable to the moderate elevation of the ground, the dryness of the atmosphere, and the absence of the fog that overspreads the valley below." Numerous examples are then given of the rich growth of flowering plants (according to E.Lees numbering 807 species) and of the trees and shrubs, many of which could not survive in less favourable conditions. Even in winter "the gardens present more of the greenness and freshness of the summer in less favoured localities."

In developing the theme of height he points out that it involves other potent hygienic considerations such as temperature, humidity, and wind currents. Malvern's merits can be seen in the following: "The height is moderate, but sufficient to isolate it from any injurious valley influences; the aspect is largely eastern, but it receives the genial warmth of the morning sun; the fall of rain may be as great as in many other places, or even greater, but it rapidly percolates the gravel and descends to the lower levels; the winds are at times boisterous, but rarely if ever as severe as in numerous other health resorts. We may content ourselves with the fact that, as a whole, the climate of Malvern is eminently hygienic." In the light of this, he argues that the moderate height of Malvern combined with other factors makes it probably even more beneficial to invalids than many of the Alpine resorts which range from upwards of 5000 feet.

Temperature, he points out, is no less important than height, and the position of Malvern in relation to the sun's rays and its shelter from cold winds make it desirable in winter as well as summer, On the one hand the aspect of Great Malvern "is south-east and its exposure to the influence of the sun and light is uninterrupted," and no less important, "its houses are built at the base and on the side of a hill which protects it from certain winds, especially the westerly, and in a large measure from the north winds. The east winds chiefly direct their influence above the elevation of the houses, at least the great proportion of them. Besides . . . the east winds of Malvern are not peculiarly cold or moist. To some extent the town is protected from descending currents of cold air by the plantations of trees which flourish on the upper slopes." Such conditions make for a moderate climate all through the year, and as evidence of this Dr Grindrod quotes statistics showing how in this respect it is superior to many other places, including for example London and Cheltenham. The absence of humidity is another valuable feature, and he attributes this partly to the fact that the houses are built on the slopes of the well wooded hills, so that such rainfall as it experiences drains away without causing excessive humidity, thus leaving Malvern free from a moist atmosphere.

Malvern water is also analysed in detail under two headings: the Chalybeate spa and the ordinary hill water of St Ann's Well and Hay Well in Great Malvern and Holy Well in Malvern Wells. Both are shown to be beneficial in their different ways, the Chalybeate because of its mineral content and the hill water because of its purity. He devotes most attention to the latter, outlining its long history of healing, applied both externally on all types of wound, and internally in the form of bottled water sent all over the country. He reminds his readers of the old song, which he dates about 1590 or 1600:

Out of that famous hill
There daily springeth
A water, passing still,
Which always bringeth
Great comfort to all them
That are diseased men,
And makes them well again
To praise the Lord . . .

A thousand bottles there
were filled weekly.
And many costrils rare,
For stomachs sickly;
Some of them unto Kent,
Some were to London sent,
Others to Berwick went –
Oh, praise the Lord.

While quoting numerous examples of cures claimed to be due to Malvern water, Dr Grindrod is guarded in his comments on the benefits that can be attributed to it: "The author has witnessed numerous cases of cure in atonic ulcers and cutaneous affections during his residence in Malvern; but whether the cure has been attributable to the air or water applications, or diet and improved nutrition, or, what is more probable, a combination of the whole, is a point which cannot always be determined. The cure, however, has been effected, and that is *the* satisfactory point to a suffering invalid."

The purity and hygienic influence of Malvern air is given his unqualified approbation: "The purity of the Malvern water depends on the perfect infiltration of the rain which pours down its hillsides through a stratum of gravelly soil, and which does not impart to it any mineral or organic principles. Malvern air is free from miasmatic influence in consequence of excellent drainage and the absence of decayed vegetable subtances, such as are found in a morass or uncultivated district. Add to these influences, what is adverted to more at length in other sections, the genial influence of a full exposure to the sun's rays, and the partial return of the heat from a receptive soil; and also the equally genial influence of not severe but stimulating winds, and the tonic results of a residence in Malvern may be fairly estimated."

The importance of ozone is then examined, and shown to be both present in the right amounts and maintained to an adequate degree throughout the year. Only occasionally due to east winds it has been for a very short time exhausted before reaching the town. "Ozone," he says, "may be characterised as Nature's deodoriser and disinfectant. A district like Malvern, where ozone is always found in abundant proportion, assuredly exhibits a remarkable absence of injurious influences."

Other factors to which he turns his attention are the electric condition of the atmosphere, exposure to sunlight, freedom from smoke, disease emanations from humans and animals, miasmatic influences, systems of drainage, and many others. In each case his conclusion is that the conditions in Malvern make it a highly desirable place for both residents and visiting patients, and he produces elaborate statistics, mainly for the years 1864-70, showing the incidence of deaths and various causes of death to prove his case. The death rate of Malvern is then compared with that in various inland and seaside watering places, and Malvern is shown to have a lower rate than "the most healthy of the marine residences and less than Leamington, Cheltenham, Matlock, Buxton, Harrogate, and others of inland repute." Further comparisons are made regarding such features as rain, humidity, and temperature in the various places under discussion.

A number of diseases are then examined. The climate of Malvern is shown to be helpful to these, in winter no less that in summer, and Dr Grindrod suggests that more should be done to advertise its winter benefits. Each type of illness is considered in great detail, and the reasons why the Malvern climate is beneficial are set out. Even for consumption he rates Malvern higher than many of the Alpine resorts because of its shelter from the east winds.

Since the book is basically concerned with climatic conditions, he devotes his end chapters to a scientific presentation of the case for supplementing the natural benefits of Malvern with the provision of a compressed air-bath to supply the exact treatment required for invalids in certain special circumstances. While nature can be trusted to furnish most of what is needed, mechanical devices have their place, and Malvern has the rare distinction of being able to provide such an appliance at Townshend House. This section of the book is a comprehensive account of his compressed air-bath and is accompanied by excellent illustrations.

15
Closing Years

Dr Grindrod's initiation into the Good Templars in the early 1870s gave an impetus to his enthusiasm for the cause of teetotalism. Besides continuing to attend their meetings he embarked on a further book on the subject, *The Nation's Vice. The Claims of Temperance on the Christian Church.* He failed however to complete it, but his son Charles, aided by a well known temperance worker, the Rev Dr Dawson Burns, undertook its revision and published it in 1884 after his father's death.

According to Charles, only minor points of revision were made. He tells us that he verified quotations, brought the statistics up to date, and changed the title from *Our National Vice* to *The National Vice* as the former title had already been used. He appears to have felt some embarrassment at the severe treatment of the clergy in the book as he drew attention to the fact that it was only in recent times that sympathy for his father's views on temperance had become widely felt. It was his conviction that if his father had lived longer he would have modified some of the material.

The main theme of the book, which is backed up by detailed statistics and anecdotal examples, is that the commercial prosperity of the nation has led to moral and social degradation, and much of this is due to "the monster evil of our day," namely alcoholic drink. Instead of battling against this evil, the Christian Church has been a powerful force promoting it, and he traces throughout its history the drinking usages that permeate its social life on such occasions as religious festivals, charitable dinners and toasts to bishops and clergy. Societies in which the Church has some influence should, he argues, move their meetings from the public house to the parochial schoolroom or to a working men's hall, and the clergy should set their face against advocating moderation instead of total abstinence, since moderation is useless in the battle against temperance. "There must," he argues, "be something in the nature of drink, distinct from that of ordinary food, to induce the inebriate appetite."

Missionary work abroad, he points out, is also damaged by the drunkenness of Christians: "To preach the Gospel of peace with the Bible in one hand and the whisky bottle in the other, however it may be the practice of modern Christians, was not the practice of Christ." At home too, "Christians have participated in those usages which have extended and deepened – if not created and fostered – our national vice." Building churches, he argues, is in the forefront of Christian activity to-day, but, he demands, "what value are they when so are public houses and gin shops, and in the proportion of three to one."

While the book is primarily directed towards the failings of the Church, Dr Grindrod does not overlook other forces at work, but to him the Church's failure is more reprehensible because Christians are "the very people who should be in the forefront of fighting against the nation's vices." "Christianity," he argues, "must conquer drink or drink will conquer Christianity."

The book repeats many arguments used earlier in *Bacchus* to contest the view that alcoholic drink is valuable both as a food and as a medicine. "Science and experience agree," he maintains, "that alcohol does not give strength;" moreover, "the statistics of insurance societies show the longevity of non-drinkers." Some of his condemnation extends beyond drinking to the habit of smoking. Members of teetotal societies should, he argues, study the other rules of health: diet, pure air, sufficient ventilation and abstinence from tobacco. Tobacco, he maintains, "is a pernicious weed which has become a national vice." It speaks well for the self-restraint of Charles that in his editorial capacity he leaves this and other stronger denunciations untouched. Charles was in fact noted for his addiction to the pipe, and in later years regularly attended the smoking concerts held by the Working Men's Institute at the Wyche. His popularity with the members was enhanced by the gifts of pipes and tobacco that he invariably made to the gathering!

In 1873 Dr Grindrod welcomed his newly qualified son into the practice at Townshend House. Charles had completed his medical course at Edinburgh and proceeded to become a licentiate of the Royal College of Physicians and the Society of Apothecaries of London. It must have given his father great pleasure that he chose to study medicine, and still more that he decided to join him at Townshend House. Besides the practice there were a number of interests that they had in common. One of these was freemasonry. Like his father, Charles became a member of Royd's Lodge, and he applied his artistic gifts to collaborate with him in designing the seal and banner used by the Lodge. The design was a combination of the seals of Great Malvern and Little Malvern Priories. Inheriting his father's skill with the pen, Charles's writings included a *Guide to Malvern*, a book of poetry, and an imaginative novel *The Shadow of the Raggedstone*, set in the Malvern area. The latter was serialised in *The Malvern Advertiser* in 1888 prior to publication.

As the only son of a man of forceful character one might have expected Charles to be moulded in the same pattern. But this was not so. He developed his own areas of interest, a main one being photography. He became the first president of the Malvern Camera Club, and his study of a girl's head entitled "Beyond" was awarded the gold medal of the Royal Photographic Society. He was much in demand for portraiture, and he included Edward Elgar among his subjects. His activities in the Society for the Preservation of Ancient Buildings and his appreciation of music were probably factors that led to his friendship with the architect Troyte Griffith who figures as Troyte in Elgar's Enigma Variations.

While his father took little interest in party politics and shunned service on committees, Charles was a keen Conservative and his interest in local politics led to his becoming in 1895 an active member of the Malvern District Council. His religious commitment was as strong as that of his father, but whereas the latter was a loyal Anglican[1] with a strong appreciation of Nonconformity because of its stance on teetotalism, Charles was wholeheartedly Anglican. When he went to live at the Wyche he took a prominent part in the building of All Saints Church, besides being a churchwarden.

It was particularly fortunate for Dr Grindrod that his son joined him in the practice, for in the mid-1870s he was becoming increasingly prone to ill health. From time to time he needed to get away for a much needed rest and Wales became a favourite place of retreat. One such occasion was in the summer of 1875, just when the season was in full swing and one would have thought it impossible for him to have taken a rest. However a letter preserved in the Malvern Museum, written by Mrs Grindrod to Charles on July 14, shows that both parents had been staying for a time in St Davids and were shortly moving on to Llandrindod Wells. After a recent visit from Charles, his father had taken to his bed and had needed treatment with leeches. He was however getting some enjoyment from his visit to Wales, as Charles was asked to post two books so that he could pursue his favourite hobbies. One was *The Geology of Wales* which his father had left on the armchair in the old dining room at Townshend House. The other was a book on the waters at Llandrindod. Money seems to have been exercising their minds. Charles is only to send the books if the postage will not exceed 1/-, and he is asked to follow up a recent debt of five guineas incurred by a patient. To spare him any embarrassment in having to ask for the money, Charles is told that the patient's mother had offered to pay and that she is wealthy.

In one respect the mid-1870s were not the best time for Charles to be embarking on the water cure in Malvern. The pioneers who had popularised it in the first place were no longer there. Dr Wilson had died suddenly in 1867 when taking the cure at the Ben Rhydding Hydro in Yorkshire, and Dr Edward Johnson who had come to Malvern in the 1850s died in the same year. While Dr Wilson's colleague and former assistant Dr Rayner took over Dr Wilson's practice at The Establishment, Malvern House which had been built as an annexe to it had become a hotel, thus limiting the number of patients that could be accommodated. In 1872 Dr Gully, who shared with Dr Wilson the distinction of being first in the field, retired and left Malvern after a long period of declining health. But it was not just the loss of such influential doctors that was causing the decline. The length of the treatment and its cost were gradually making the cure less acceptable, and the Spartan regime in so many of the practices was proving a deterrent. In spite of this general waning of interest Dr Grindrod seems still to have had faith in its future. As late as 1879 he embarked on costly improvements to Townshend House, the emphasis being on bringing the furnishings up to date. A typical example of the change is described in the article in *The Malvern Advertiser* (October 11,1879): "Passing through a well-kept green-house we enter the House through a passage laid with tessellated tiles of the most recent make; and entering the rooms which lie along the passage we see at once that they have all been newly furnished . . . the drawing room is elegantly and tastefully fitted with all the appliances of modern furnishing . . ." There is however at least a hint that there has been some decline in the house's fortunes, but the article ends with the emphasis on future prospects: "We anticipate a greatly revived future for Townshend House, with the additions and improvements which have just been made. Though effected somewhat late in the season, there has been a large number of visitors at Townshend House this year – the depressed state of commerce notwithstanding – than has been the case for several preceding years. Of one thing we are sure, were the Establishment half as well known as we know it, every room in it would be occupied from year's end to year's end."

Unfortunately by now Dr Grindrod's health was rapidly deteriorating and severe heart trouble forced him to retire. Leaving his son in charge to wind up affairs he moved to Carlsruhe on the Wells Road and later lived for a time in Wales. By 1881 Charles had moved with his wife to Wyche-Side in Malvern Wells, and Townshend House was on the market. A discussion of its future in the *Advertiser* (December 17) observes that "If Townshend House should once more be resuscitated, it will be in a very attractive style and will be among the very best houses in the kingdom. With the surroundings of its beautiful scenery, its pure air and equable temperature, and above all its matchless water, it should outvie every place seized upon by medical practitioners to aid them in the all-important work of healing." Unfortunately it failed to find a buyer prepared to give it such a future and it was not until 1886 that the house was sold. In that year it was bought by the Rev Dr William Walker, a schoolmaster from Reading, who opened it in May 1888 as Connellan College. In 1891 it became the property of the English Benedictines from St Edmund's Douai, and finally Malvern College acquired it in a period of post-war expansion in 1919. In view of Dr Grindrod's many years of friendly association with the college this seems an appropriate ending to its story.

The sale of the museum went through much more speedily. So many leading geologists and palaeontologists had shown an interest in it in earlier years that when it was put on the market in 1882 there was competition to acquire it. Dr Grindrod's legal adviser, Mr John Thompson of Pierpoint Street, Worcester, was given the task of conducting negotiations and he appointed Professor Etheridge of the British Museum (Natural History) to value the collection. Besides sending his report to Mr Thompson he wrote at length to Professor Prestwich who he knew was interested in obtaining the collection for the Oxford University Museum.[2] Although Dr Grindrod and his adviser were aware that a much higher sum could be obtained if the collection were split up and sold to dealers (estimated at £1500 to £1600), Dr Grindrod, who was primarily interested in its educational value was insistent that it should be sold as a unity. Both Professor Etheridge and others who saw it at this time were unanimous in their praise of its contents. He expressed this in a letter to Professor Prestwich, dated October 7, 1882: "Neither Oxford or any other place will ever see the like again;" and this observation applied both to the fossils that had been gathered locally and other collections which Dr Grindrod had bought from further afield. He was particularly impressed with the Trilobites, and assured Mr Thompson that these were "extremely fine (upwards of 500) – some of these are unique." Professor Blake of University College, Nottingham concurred with this view of the importance of the collection, particularly in regard to the cephalopoda on which he was working: "It is a collection which should not on any account be scattered as it has taken years to collect with the most unique opportunities and at an expense far greater than the price asked. I only examined critically the cephalopoda which themselves seemed lost amidst the wealth of Trilobites and other specimens, but such was the beauty and uniqueness of the fossils of this group that for the illustration of my Vol 1 of the British cephalopoda. I spent more than £50 on the drawing of them alone, they contributing more than a fifth part of the whole and including the majority of the unique or rarest specimens."

While Professor Etheridge recommended to Mr Thompson a valuation of £420 on contents, or a total of £500 to include display cabinets, he stressed that this was not a true estimate of their real value. In his communication of this to Professor Etheridge, Mr Thompson added his own comment: "This view according to the opinions expressed to me by numerous persons acquainted with Geology does not but in a very small degree represent <u>the intrinsic value</u> of this collection. The cases are included in the amount named but I am informed that they cost originally about £300 ... The Institution or person who may now acquire this Collection will be very fortunate in securing a "Treasure" <u>and</u> at the price a "great bargain.""

Much of the correspondence on the sale was concerned with the cabinets. Professor Etheridge referred to the main cabinet as "extremely fine, valuable and suited to any museum being <u>in the best of taste</u> plain solid oak & over 300 drawers beneath the top glass part. It <u>must have cost £150</u> with the cabinet." Mr Thompson described the size of both cabinets: "The principal case is 46 feet long, 4ft 6 in. wide and about 4ft high in the centre – the whole of the top is glazed so as to shew the specimens placed at the top and in the underpart there are upwards of 300 drawers. Besides this there is a small upright case placed against the wall which is 5ft 10 in. wide and about 8 feet high." It was not intended that they should be sold separately from the contents, and accordingly the total sum asked and paid was £500, the successful bidder being Professor Prestwich for the Oxford University Museum. Among others who put in bids were the MP for Worcester, Mr Rowley Hill, who wanted to secure it for a local museum, and Professor Geikie who represented the Glasgow Museum. The British Museum (Natural History) would have welcomed it, but unfortunately a recent expensive acquisition had left it too financially drained to make a firm offer. Professor Blake expressed a wish to acquire some of the duplicates for the University College of Nottingham, but there was no question of any partial sales at this stage.

The very large number of duplicates had caused problems for Professor Etheridge's attempt at valuation, and an interesting comment by him throws light on Dr Grindrod as a collector: "the Duplicates are of course numerous as would be expected from a man like Grindrod who obtained everything." Consequently the arrangement and cataloguing seems to have left something to be desired: "There are <u>8000</u> specimens I know, <u>probably</u> 10,000. Had they been named & classified & localized <u>I know not what sum may have been put upon them</u>." If quantity and quality were characteristic of Dr Grindrod as a collector they were no less typical of his whole way of life. Whether he was campaigning for temperance, practising as a doctor, or planning the extension and refurbishment of his home, he threw himself totally into each task, and no expense was spared in his commitment to the best.

It must have saddened Dr Grindrod that because of ill health he was unable to supervise the sale of the museum but he would have been pleased at its outcome. In the following year he and Mrs Grindrod returned from Wales and took rented accommodation at The Ruby, Malvern Wells, not far from Wyche-Side where Charles now had his practice. The advertisement of The Ruby in *Malvern Illustrated* describes its amenities: "This old-established Lodging-House is very pleasantly situated, and commands magnificent views of the Severn Valley. Within easy distance are the Golf Links, the British Camp, the Holy Well, and the Midland and Great Western Railway Stations. Brakes pass every half- hour. Private access to the Hills, and an unlimited supply of the purest spring water." Its proprietor George Smith stated that its terms were moderate. Here they stayed until Dr Grindrod's death on November 18,1883.

The funeral took place at St Peter's Malvern Wells, conducted by the Vicar, the Rev R.F.S. Perfect and the Rev C.L.Banister of the Wyche, and attended by the relatives and many friends. Clergy, doctors, schoolmasters and local businessmen were well represented. He was buried in St Peter's churchyard, his grave marked by a massive stone cross. The inscription included the name, dates of birth and death, and a brief text "A Servant of Jesus Christ, Complete in Him." Mrs Grindrod, who spent her last years with her son, died five years later on 11 March 1888 and was buried in the same grave, with a further inscription "Them also who sleep in Jesus will God bring with Him".

Among the early obituaries were those in the *Church of England Temperance Chronicle*, the *Alliance News* and the *Manchester Guardian*, which acknowledged its debt to the latter. These drew attention to the breadth of Dr Grindrod's interests, but concentrated on his pioneer temperance work in Manchester and throughout the country, and cited some of his leading contacts in this field, notably Dr Stanley, Bishop of Norwich, and John Cassell, founder of the by then well-known publishing firm. *The Church of England Temperance Chronicle* quoted extensively from Dr Grindrod's personal reminiscences published some months earlier in the *British Temperance Advocate*, which gave valuable insight into the demanding nature of his medical temperance mission. Its author Frederick Sherlock noted that the wide acceptance at the present time of the argument that the use of alcoholic drinks is inimical to health had come about largely as a result of "the enlightened teaching and persevering advocacy of Dr Grindrod, who fifty years ago stood almost alone among his professional brethren as a supporter of the Temperance Movement."

The obituary in *The Malvern Advertiser* included much of the same material but gave more detail on the role of Townshend House as a hydropathic establishment which was unique in being also a centre of philanthropic and educational work. On a more personal note the writer said of him: "Dr Grindrod had a large heart," and this statement is expanded with the tribute: "In all efforts to benefit society, especially among the working classes, he was sure to be found, and his advocacy was always enlisted on the part of the poor and helpless." Such a comment would have been endorsed by one of his early Malvern patients, Paxton Hood, who said of him: "He is in truth, a most loveable and delightful man. He lives for his patients, and in the study of their state, their wants and their comforts, and all love him and trust him. He is a most generous-hearted and liberal-minded man."[3]

Notes

Chapter 1

1 Dr Grindrod's gravestone has Swettenham cum Kermincham and his baptismal certificate has Swettenham, but I have followed his own preference in naming Kermincham as his place of birth (e.g.census records 1861, 1871). It seems unlikely that he would have specifically mentioned the smaller place if his claim were not valid.

2 The name Grindrod is first attested in Rochdale in 1541 with the spelling Greenroade (OE grēne = grass, and rod = clearing)

Chapter 2

1 A.Redford. *History of Local Government in Manchester*. Vol 2, p19f.

2 Alexis de Tocqueville. *Journeys to England and Ireland*. ed J.P. Meyer 1958, p136.

3 *Mary Barton*. Chapter 6.

Chapter 3

1 P.T.Winskill. *The Temperance Movement and its Workers*. Vol 1. Chapter 1X.

Chapter 4

1 T. Swindells. *Manchester Streets and Manchester Men*. Vol 1. p159.

2 P.T.Winskill. *The Temperance Movement and its Workers*. Vol 1. Chapter 1X.

3 Marriage Certificate August 30,1837, Collegiate Church in the Parish of Manchester, gives John Hull as Worsted Dealer and Dr Grindrod's father as Gentleman.

Chapter 5

1 P.T.Winskill.*Comprehensive History of the Rise and Progress of the Temperance Reformation*. p51.

Chapter 6

1 *The Temperance Movement and its Workers.* Vol 1. Chapter XXV111.

2 See 1 above.

Chapter 7

1 T.Cook. *National Temperance Magazine.* May-December 1845.

2 Quoted in *Church of England Temperance Chronicle* obit 24.11.83. from earlier article in the *British Temperance Advocate.*

3 See 2 above.

Chapter 8

1 *The Temperance News.* Vol 1. Nos 1-8. 1846.

2 *Comprehensive History of the Temperance Movement.* p505.

Chapter 9

1 There is no consistency in the spelling of its name. Townshend is probably used more often, but Dr Grindrod himself frequently writes Townsend.

Chapter 11

1 *British Medical Journal,* October 12,1861, and October 26,1861.

2 George Wilson Papers, November 27,1869. Letter M20/30. Manchester Public Library.

Chapter 12

1 *The Temperance Movement and its Workers.* Vol 3. p198-9.

2 *The Templar,* April 23,1874.

Chapter 13

1 A mistake occurs in the entry. Cleevely indicates that Dr Grindrod flourished 1895, but he must have confused him with his son as Dr Grindrod died in 1883.

2 *Health and Pleasure or Malvern Punch,* p106f.

3 The correct term is Beyrichia.

4 *The Metropolis of the Water Cure.* p132.
5 This was a variety named by J.W.Salter in 1864 as *Phacops (Odontochiele) caudatus varß Grindrodianus.* Others that bear his name are *Acanthopleurella Grindrodi* and *Prantlia (Malvernocare) Grindrodi.* Among Cephalopoda, J.F.Blake lists *Orthoceras Grindrodi.*

Chapter 15
1 He regularly attended Anglican services, and for two years, 1853 and 1854, was churchwarden at Malvern Priory. The probable reason for giving up is that he was about to launch *The Malvern Advertiser.* As the Priory was engaged on a heavy programme of restoration under Sir Gilbert Scott he may well have felt that he could not manage both commitments.
2 To-day his fossils share house-room in the Oxford University Museum of Natural History with some fine skeletons of dinosaurs.
3 *The Metropolis of the Water Cure.* Letter 3.

Sources of Information

Original Records and Documents

Bodleian MS. D.D.Dew

Census Returns, Manchester and Malvern, 1841-91

Chorlton Row Dispensary Reports, 1826-32

George Wilson Archives M20/30,1869. Manchester City Reference Library, Local Studies

Grindrod, Dr R. B. Marriage Certificate, August 30, 1837. Collegiate Church in Parish of Manchester

Grindrod, Dr R. B. Death Certificate, November 18, 1883. Sub-District of Hanley Castle

Guildhall Library, London. S.Freeth MSS 8241/3, 8241/5, 8241/23

Oxford University Museum of Natural History: Letters re Dr Grindrod's Museum

Malvern Museum: Letter from Mrs Grindrod to Charles Grindrod

Worcester Record Office. Malvern Priory Records Box 7

Newspapers, Journals and Directories

Alliance News, 1881

British Medical Journal, September & October 1861

Church of England Temperance Chronicle, November 24,1883

Doncaster Gazette, August 15, 22, 1881

Journal of Medical Biography, 1997, 5. M.L.Crosfill: *Dr R.B. Grindrod, the Medical Apostle of Temperance*

The Lancet, 1855

The Malvern Advertiser

The Malvern News

National Temperance Magazine,Vol2, 1845

Provincial Medical & Surgical Journal, 1844, 1847

Temperance Jubilee Celebrations, compiled by T.Cook, November 13-18, 1886. T.Cook Travel Archives

The Temperance News, Vol 1,1846

The Templar, 1874

Pigot & Sons: Manchester Directory, 1838
Pigot & Slater: Manchester and Salford Directory, 1841
P.O.Directory of Southampton and Neighbourhood, 1843f

Books and Pamphlets

Axon: *Annals of Manchester*

J.F.Blake: *Monograph of the British Fossil Cephalopoda*, Part 1. J.Van Voorst 1882

Piers Brendan: *Thomas Cook*. Secker & Warburg 1991

E.M.Brockbank: *The Hon. Medical Staff of the Manchester Royal Infirmary*. 1836, reprinted 1965

E.M.Brockbank: *The Foundations of Provincial Medical Education in England*. Manchester University Press 1936

J.Burns (J.B.Oddfish): *Health and Pleasure or Malvern Punch*. Simpkin, Marshall & Co 1865

R.J.Cleevely: *World Palaeontological Collections*. 1983

R.A.Fortey: *Trilobite!* Harper Collins 2000

A.B.Granville: *The Spas of England, South Division*. Henry Colburn 1841

J.Grierson; *Dr Wilson and his Malvern Hydro*. Cora Weaver 1998

R.B.Grindrod: *Bacchus*, 1839

"   "   *The Wrongs of our Youth*, 1843, (Reprinted 1972 Harvard Graduate School of Business Administration)

R.B.Grindrod: *The Slaves of the Needle*, 1844, (Reprinted 1972 Harvard)

"   "   *The Compressed Air Bath*, 1860

"   "   *Malvern Past and Present*, 1865

"   "   *Malvern: Its Claims as a Health Resort*

"   "   *The Nation's Vice*, Edited by C.F.Grindrod 1884

R.Hall-Jones: *A Malvern Bibliography*. First Paige 1988

J.W.Harcup: *The Malvern Water Cure*

B.H.Harrison: *Drink and the Victorians*. Faber & Faber 1971

M.C.Hodgetts: Malvern Naturalists' Field Club.

P. Hood: *The Metropolis of the Water Cure*. Simpkin Marshall & Co 1858

Malvern Writers' Circle: *Write Around Malvern* (article, Cora Weaver) 1984

Manchester City News, *Notes and Queries*, Vol2. 1879

R.I.Murchison: *Siluria*. John Murray 1859

ed. Open University: *Industry and Culture* 1830-1914. Macmillan 1970

J.V. Pickstone: *Medicine and Industrial Society: a History of Hospital Development in Manchester and its Region.* Manchester University Press 1985

A.Redford; *History of Local Government in Manchester*, Vol2. Longmans Green 1940

T.Rigby: *A History of Runcorn and Weston*

J.W.Salter: *A Monograph of the British Trilobites from the Cambrian, Silurian and Devonian Formations.* Palaeontographical Publications 1864-83

T.Swindells: *Manchester Streets and Manchester Men.* 1906

K.A.Webb: *The Development of the Medical Profession in Manchester 1750-1860.* Thesis, University of Manchester 1988

J.Wheeler: *Manchester: its Political, Social, and Commercial History.* Whittaker & Co 1836

P.T.Winskill: *Comprehensive History of the Rise & Progress of the Temperance Reformation* 1881

    "   *The Temperance Movement and its Workers.* Blackie 1891

    "   *Temperance Standard Bearers.* 1897

Woolhope Naturalists' Field Club. 1866

Index